# The CEO'S Guide to

# MARKETING

Published by Maple Island
Burnsville, MN
www.Publicity.com

Copyright ©2017 Media Relations Agency

Distributed by Greenleaf Book Group

For ordering information or special discounts for bulk purchases, please contact Greenleaf Book Group at PO Box 91869, Austin, TX  78709, 512.891.6100.

Design by Katie Hanson at Checkerboard.com.

Cataloging-in-Publication data is available.

Print ISBN: 978-0-9990693-0-1

eBook ISBN: 978-0-9990693-1-8

Printed in China

17 18 19 20 21 22   10 9 8 7 6 5 4 3 2 1
First Edition

# The CEO'S Guide to
# MARKETING

The most practical marketing book you will ever read

Introducing The **SAM6**™ Process

## 6 STEPS to more LEADS higher SALES and a stronger BRAND

## by Lonny Kocina

Maple Island

# TABLE OF CONTENTS

We've created a set of online tools to help you as you work through the SAM 6™ process. You can find these tools and more at **publicity.com.**

## Note

*When talking about marketing, it's considered an acceptable shortcut to combine both products and services, and just use the word product. It makes conversation easier. Sort of like asking a group of friends, "Hey, you guys wanna to go to a movie?" rather than, "Hey, you males, females, adults and children wanna to go to a movie?" So when product is mentioned throughout this book, remember it means both products and services.*

## Start Here

The premise of this book is simple. Most people in marketing, from the top on down, know a lot less about marketing than they let on. Many don't even know the basics of marketing, and it's unfortunate how much money is being wasted and sales missed over something that is relatively easy to solve. The CEO's Guide to Marketing will show CEOs, as well as their marketing teams, an easy-to-understand six-step process I call Strategically Aimed Marketing, or for short: the SAM 6 process. The SAM 6 process will increase the results of your marketing dramatically. It will take a little effort for marketers to learn and implement the six steps of Strategically Aimed Marketing, but—and this is the CEO coming out in me—too bad. No company would put up with an accountant who didn't know proper accounting, and no company should put up with a marketer who doesn't know proper marketing.

What makes me an expert? I began my career as a commercial artist and was promoted to marketing director at a company with sales in the hundreds of millions. That was back when you could still smoke in the office and no one had a computer. Then in 1986, I started Media Relations Agency. Over the years we have served several hundred clients which means we get a behind-the-scenes look at the inner workings of marketing in many, many companies. In addition to running the agency, for fun I sometimes teach Principles of Marketing at the college level. I've spent my whole life in marketing and made millions along the way. So, I've learned a few things I can teach CEOs or anyone else who wants to learn.

I'm not an ivory tower academic or someone born with a silver spoon. I'm a pretty regular guy who speaks plainly. Even though this book is filled with marketing terms and concepts, I have tried to write in a way that makes them easy to understand.

Whether you are a CEO, or someone else ambitious enough to pick up this book, like a marketing manager, graphic artist, web designer, writer, photographer, publicist, or anyone else who has a hand in creating promotions–degree or no degree, you are about to become the smartest marketer in the room.

## Let's get to work

I want you to keep this in mind while you read along: **Marketing is not *about* fun. It just happens to *be* fun. Marketing is about the shortest, fastest, least expensive and most direct route to a lead, a sale and a brand.**

What drives me crazy is too many marketers jump right to the fun part of creating promotions. It's nice that marketing isn't drudgery like some jobs, but there is a process that needs to be followed long before the creative fun begins. And if the creativity comes before the process, it really screws things up. And that's what most companies seem to have: screwed up marketing.

The Strategically Aimed Marketing process will prevent needless chaos and assure creative people stay focused, on track and doing their best work.

The six steps of the Strategically Aimed Marketing process (maybe it would be more accurate to call them sequential facets) are Competence, Code, Channels, Calendar, Control and Creative. The first and last step are like bookends to the other four steps. Step 1, Competence, is becoming clear about what marketing is and understanding why you need to know key marketing terms. Step 6. Creative, is about assembling the team you will need to execute your marketing. Steps 2, 3, 4 and 5, lay a foundation for creative ideation. Together the six steps (or facets) produce better marketing results.

As a CEO, you don't have to worry much about creativity. That happens naturally in marketing. What you want to focus on, and what the SAM 6 process is about, is developing a consistent repeatable process that will produce more leads, higher sales and a stronger brand.

The six steps of Strategically Aimed Marketing, like the hood that covers the engine of your car, are deceptively simple on the surface.

Before I begin explaining the intricacies of each step in detail, I want you to look at a couple images that will help you grasp the overview of the SAM 6 process. Think of Strategically Aimed Marketing as a *model*, a *method* and a *process*.

The SAM 6 *model* looks like this:

The SAM 6 *method* is explained in this book:

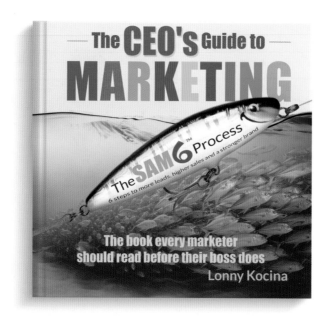

And the SAM 6 *process* is your organization going through each step as outlined in the model and explained in the book.

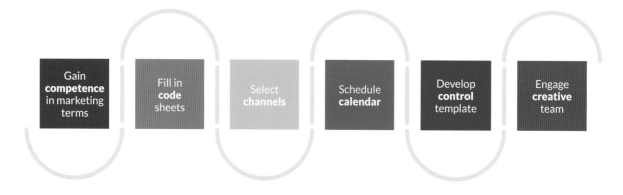

If you scan the book you might be tempted to go right to the second step. But don't. Read the first step first.

The first step in the SAM 6 process, **Competence**, is to wrap your mind around what marketing is. I'll make that clear for you in the next few pages.

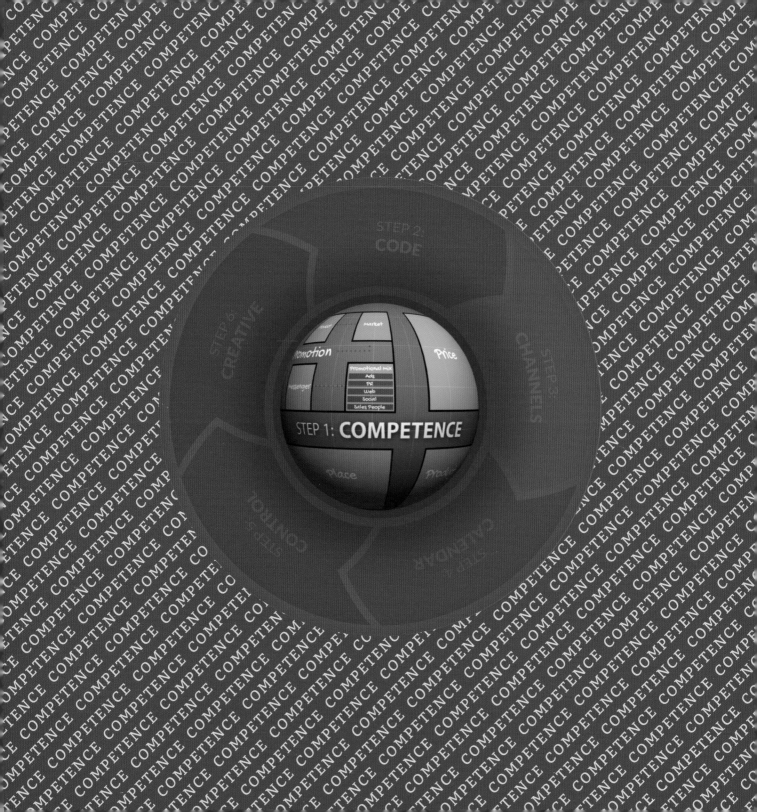

# COMPETENCE

## CHAPTERS

1 2 3

Who needs to know these terms and how can we teach them?

Wouldn't it be great if we all spoke the same marketing language?

Let's develop some tests so we can benchmark our knowledge.

Gain **competence** in marketing terms

Fill in **code** sheets

Select **channels**

Schedule **calendar**

Develop **control** template

Engage **creative** team

Implementing the
**SAM 6 Process**

# 1

# A Birdseye View

Gain
**competence**
in marketing
terms

1

Fill in
**code**
sheets

# 1 A Birdseye View

Everything that is marketing can be organized into a simple, easy-to-remember structure. Why is knowing the structure of marketing important? Because without the structure, marketing is confusing and murky. With it, marketing is organized and clear.

I'll start my explanation using a floor plan as a metaphor and then we'll wrap that floorplan around a globe which I call Planet Marketing.

Your home is made up of many rooms and compartments. That way, you don't have to keep every kind of household item in one big open space. Imagine how much frustration you would feel if you kept hairbrushes, dog food, shoes, silverware, power tools and pillows all in the same room. That's what marketing feels like when you aren't clear on the structure: a mess.

Grasping the structure of marketing enables you to mentally store the details of marketing in the right "rooms". This is useful in many ways, such as strategizing in your head, conducting a meeting with staff or vendors, and writing a marketing plan.

I'm going to combine three marketing terms that will provide you with a helpful mental image. Two of the terms are standard marketing terms: the Marketing Mix and the Promotional Mix. The other term is one I came up with and call the Promotional Sequence. First, I will explain the terms, and then I will combine them.

I apologize if the first couple pages are too basic for some but read them anyway. It won't hurt you.

# The Marketing Mix

Understanding the structure of marketing begins with the most basic term in marketing, the Marketing Mix. The Marketing Mix simply divides marketing into four quadrants: Product, Price, Place and Promotion.

**Product** is anything that has to do with creating the product, service or offering. **Price** is anything to do with determining the price consumers will ultimately pay for the product, service or offering. **Place** can be thought of as distribution. It is the place where the product resides at any given time. **Promotion** refers to getting the word out to consumers.

In most companies, <u>Promotion is the primary job of marketing</u>. Marketing may play a role in *Product* development but that's usually the responsibility of research and development. *Price* is normally a function of accounting, and much of *Place* is handled by logistics.

In most companies, Promotion is the primary job of marketing.
(We'll cover that soon)

## The Promotional Sequence

There are six categories in the Promotional Sequence: company, product, market, message, messenger and promotional mix.

The Promotional Sequence is stated like this: A **company** creates a **product** that it sells to a **market** using a **message** said by a **messenger** through **promotional mix** channels.

It can also be said in reverse order: The **promotional mix** is made up of channels through which the **messenger** delivers a **message** to a **market** about a **product** on behalf of a **company**.

The first five categories in the Promotional Sequence, **company** through **messenger**, are where your planning and strategy take place.

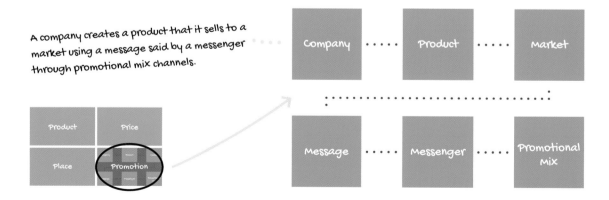

A company creates a product that it sells to a
market using a message said by a messenger
through promotional mix channels.

# The Promotional Mix

Your strategizing and planning will be put to the test when the message is finally delivered to consumers. That happens in the last category of the Promotional Sequence: the Promotional Mix. The Promotional Mix consists of five channels: Publicity, Website, Social Media, Advertising and Personal Selling.

Of the thousands of ways you can promote your product, almost all of them fit neatly into one of the Promotional Mix channels. The Promotional Mix is where the rubber meets the road. It's one thing to imagine that you have created a product your market desires; it's another when you put your message to the test by engaging with real people.

The Promotional Mix consists of five channels: Publicity, Website, Social Media, Advertising and Personal Selling.

When you combine the previous terms and graphics, you get a nice birdseye view of the structure of marketing. You can see it looks similar to the floor plan of a home. That's why I like that analogy when I teach people about the structure of marketing. The nice thing is, everything in marketing fits into one of these "rooms". Go ahead and try to think of something related to marketing that doesn't fit.

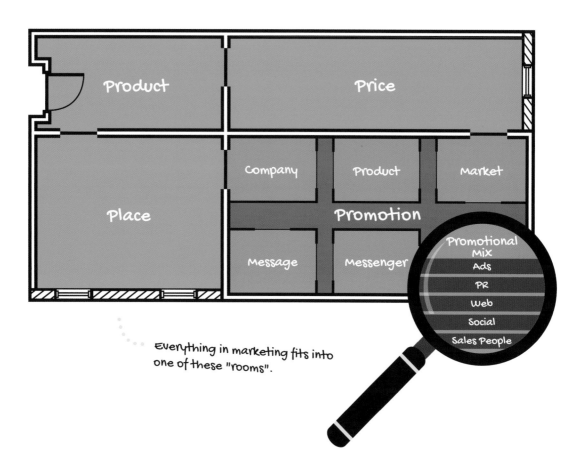

Everything in marketing fits into one of these "rooms".

While I like the floor plan analogy, it doesn't go quite far enough. That's why I wrap the floor plan around a globe and call it Planet Marketing. I've been told my planet analogy is a step too far, but it works for me, so I'm including it. What I'm trying to point out is, like the earth, marketing *is* what it *is* and it's *not* what it's *not*. No one is confused about what the earth is and isn't. Understanding marketing should be just as clear. Everyone should know where they are on Planet Marketing at any given moment.

On Planet Marketing, the rooms become continents, countries and states. The Marketing Mix is four continents. The Promotional Sequence becomes six countries. And the country of Promotional Mix has five states.

Marketing loses a lot of its mystique once you memorize and grasp this visual.

The next time you are in a marketing meeting or strategizing in your head, practice referring back to the floor plan or planet graphic. You'll be able to see exactly where you are within the scope of marketing.

Holding a visual in your mind, such as a floor plan or planet, will give you the upper hand in marketing meetings. You'll see that as people are talking, most don't have a clue where they are on Planet Marketing. They skip around randomly as one thought leads to another. But if you hold this image in your mind, you'll know where they are. That means you will be able to guide the conversation, keep meetings on track, and make sure marketing processes run smoothly.

I've seen people use the general confusion many feel about marketing to their advantage. If the whole group is lost in the woods, who's to say the person talking the loudest doesn't know the way out. As you read along in this book, you should gain a quiet confidence that will keep these forceful personalities from steering you in the wrong direction.

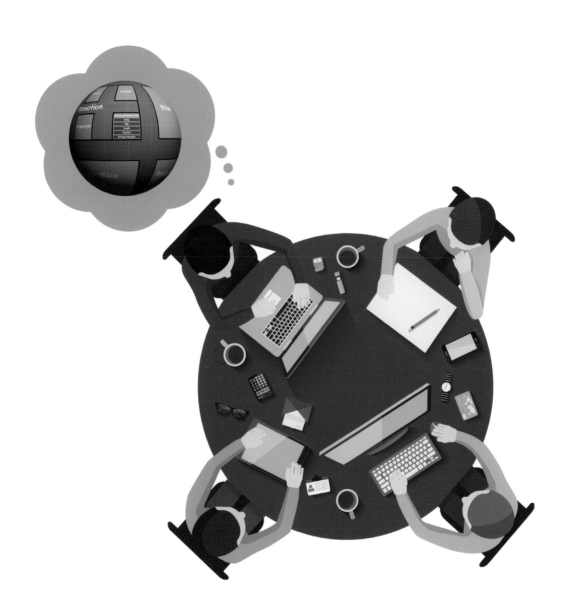

# 2

# The Importance of Terms

Gain **competence** in marketing terms

2

Fill in **code** sheets

# 2  The Importance of Terms

As I mentioned on the back cover of this book, it might surprise you to learn that many marketers (actually most) don't know basic marketing terms. You won't find this in other industries. Dentists know bicuspids from incisors. Lawyers know affidavits from briefs. Architects know cornices from parapets. But most marketers wouldn't know a push from a pull strategy if a bass boat filled with tortilla chips bit them in the butt. (If you don't get the joke, you will by the time you're finished with this book.)

At Media Relations Agency, we came up with a system to make sure every employee knows marketing terms. It's simple, effective and you can use it too. Here's how it works.

You will notice there is a term section at the back of this book with 31 terms (including the six steps of the SAM 6 process), one for each day of the month. We start every meeting, all day long, with the marketing term of the day. For instance, term number 14 is Market Segmentation Strategies. So on the 14th of each month, every meeting begins by discussing how that term applies to the work we are doing. If someone happens to be in three meetings on the 14th, they will discuss Market Segmentation Strategies three times. Day after day, month after month, year after year, these terms become ingrained in everyone's mind at our Agency.

I think you will find our system handy as you incorporate the SAM 6 process into your organization. The terms in the back of the book are the ones we use at Media Relations Agency. You can use ours or do some research and come up with your own. (By the way, we also have a list of traits we value at our agency, and we cycle through those at the same time.) I love it when someone pipes up and says, "Hey, we forgot to start our meeting with our marketing terms and traits we value."

I have an interesting story that's kind of fun and helped me understand the importance of marketing terms, so I thought I would share it.

I was reading the book *Objectivist Epistemology* by Ayn Rand when I came across an intriguing little experiment. Rand was a writer and philosopher. *Objectivism* was her philosophy and *epistemology* is the theory of knowledge. Anyway, there was some research done to see if crows could count. The experiment went like this. The researchers found an open field with a clump of trees in the middle. They put a pile

of corn next to the clump of trees and got some crows used to feeding on it. Then, they sent one researcher over to hide in the clump of trees. Naturally, the crows flew off and didn't return until the researcher left. Next, they sent two researchers to hide in the trees. Then sent one back. The crows knew two people were hiding and only one person went back so they stayed away until the second person left. They repeated this with three people, and then four. When the researchers got to four, the crows couldn't keep track. They sent four people to hide in the clump of trees, three went back, and the crows came back to feed not realizing there was still one person hiding near the corn.

The conclusion was that crows can count to three but not four.

On an observational level, humans are not much smarter than crows. They can observe up to about seven without counting. If you did your own little experiment and had someone look at nine oranges on a table, without counting them, and then took one away while they weren't watching, you'd find they couldn't tell the difference. This becomes even more obvious as quantities increase. Without counting, it would be impossible for a person to tell the difference between a group of 217 oranges and a group of 218.

What makes humans smarter than crows is our use of words and numbers as placeholders for concepts which exist independent of the word or number. Let's examine for a moment the first few words in the sentence; *Every word is a label for a complex concept.* **Every** means all things, not just one, or two or most. And it's usually all items in a particular set of items, like every fork on the table. **Word** is the term we use for the labels we put on concepts. Words can be spoken or written. They are made from the 26 letters, some of which are vowels that have hard and soft sounds as they are spoken. Words can also be expressed in many different languages. **Is**, is the act of being. It's singular and it means something exists, but not always because you can say a Martian is green and we all know Martians don't exist.

Marketers need to know marketing terms so you can think and communicate with others about marketing fast.

How amazing is it that your mind is now processing the words you are reading at the rate of 250 to 300 words per minute. Your ability to recognize and assimilate words at lightning speed is astounding. Until, of course, you come to a word you aren't familiar with. It's there that the thinking process comes to a screeching halt.

For instance, would you rather be bitten by a Hymenoptera or a Diptera? Unless you were paying close attention in your seventh-grade science class, you might mistakenly say Hymenoptera, which is the class wasps and bees fall into, rather than Diptera which is mosquitoes and flies.

As a marketer, you need to know marketing terms so you can think and communicate with others about marketing fast. Once you memorize and internalize marketing terms, you will be surprised at how fast you can think about marketing, and if others know them, how quick and indepth your conversations become. You'll notice as you read along that I use and explain some of these terms to help teach the concepts in the SAM 6 process.

# 3

# Branding

Gain **competence** in marketing terms

3

Fill in **code** sheets

# 3 Branding

Before we move on to step 2, Code, I want to be clear about one term: **Brand**. It's difficult to imagine someone being competent in marketing and being confused about the term Brand.

In my opinion, Brand is the most misused term in marketing. Many people use the word Brand as a synonym for their product or company. That may be ok if your product or company is known by everyone in the market, but most aren't. My advice is don't call your product or company your brand. It diminishes the importance of the word and deludes you into thinking you have accomplished something you haven't.

Agencies also misuse the term Brand as a way of puffing up their services. A pet peeve of mine is when agencies create guidelines for the use of a company's logo, color scheme and type fonts, and charge a handsome fee by calling it a "brand book". Don't be fooled. That's not a brand book. That's a *style guide*. They may do a little tagline work and identify some key messages but the outcome is usually just a glorified style guide.

In addition to being misused, the term Brand is also misunderstood. Most textbook and dictionary definitions of a brand go something like this: A *brand is a name, term, symbol or design that distinguishes one seller's products from another.* That's not a brand. That's a logo. Wikipedia used to have the same definition. At the time of this writing, it's been updated to a convoluted description I'm not sure anyone could understand.

Here's what I consider the right definition of Brand:

**A brand is the definition people hold in their minds of your company and the products (or services) it offers. A brand is built in two ways: by what you tell people and by what they experience.**

That's the bullseye of marketing: creating messages that build the correct definition in people's minds.

Branding is about shaping people's thinking. Your marketing communications need to form a definition so clear and strong that it causes people to want whatever it is you are offering more than whatever it is they have to give up to get it—usually money or time. Both are precious commodities.

Most CEOs think their companies and products are best-kept secrets. They feel that if everyone just knew how great their companies and products were, everybody would buy. Marketing closes the gap between people not knowing about your products and knowing about them. That's branding, and it's not easy.

Imagine you are the brand manager for a major fast food chain. You are the person responsible for the definition people all across the world hold in their minds. Now ask 20 people how they would define your company and its products. You'll likely get 20 different answers. Some favorable and some not so favorable. One person might tell you their kids love going there. Another might say they hate their greasy food. Someone else might say they love the fries. Still another might mention their charity work.

As a marketer, you have a big job. Good luck getting everyone to think about your company and products exactly as you would like them to. But that's the challenge. So, let's roll up our sleeves and get on to step 2, where we will create code sheets that will be the basis for all your promotional messages.

If you ask 20 people how they define a major fast food chain and its products you will likely get 20 different answers.

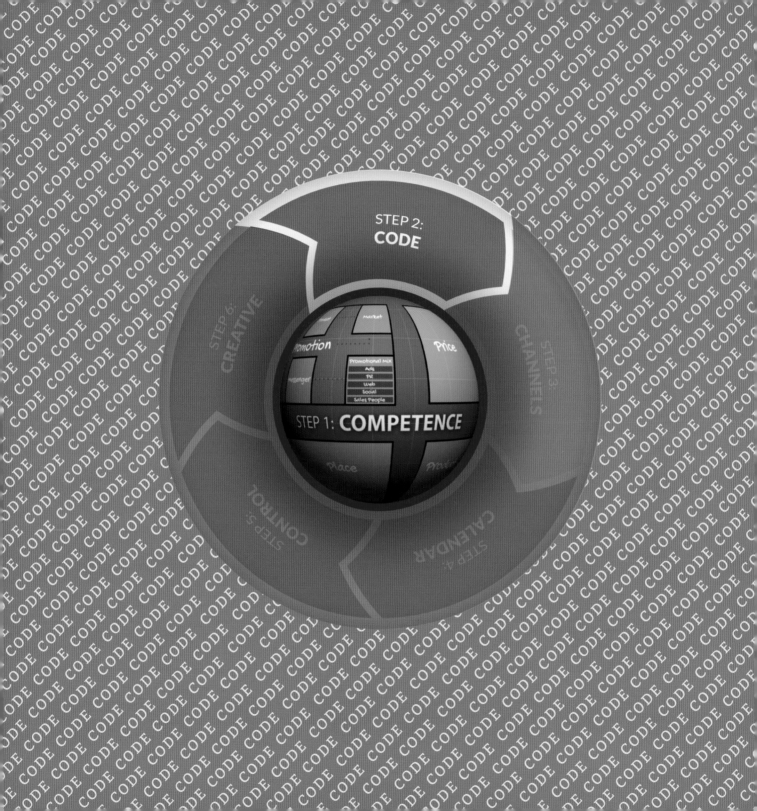

## STEP 2

# CODE

**CHAPTERS**

| 4 | 5 | 6 | 7 | 8 | 9 | 10 | 11 | 12 | 13 | 14 | 15 | 16 |

Code sheets will help us agree on what's important to our customers.

It will be great to have all this information in one place.

Let's set up a meeting to discuss product value point message themes.

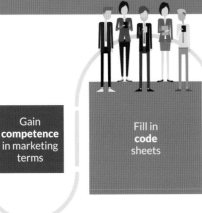

| Gain **competence** in marketing terms | Fill in **code** sheets | Select **channels** | Schedule **calendar** | Develop **control** template | Engage **creative** team |

Implementing the
**SAM 6 Process**

# 4

# Code

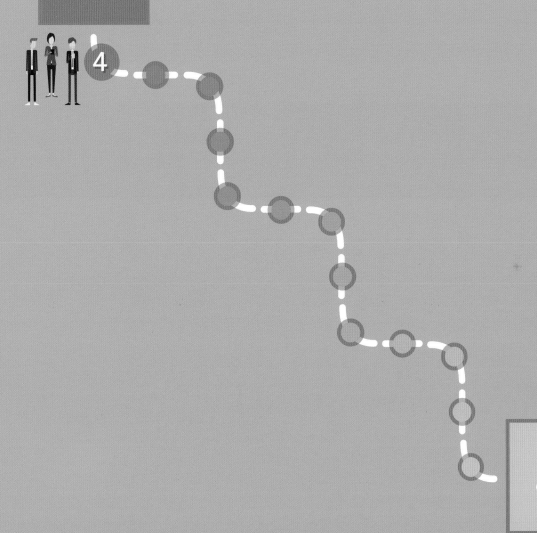

Fill in
**code**
sheets

4

Select
**channels**

# 4    Code

Creating your promotional messages begins with understanding another basic marketing concept: the Communication Process. The Communication Process goes like this: **A sender encodes a message that is decoded by the receiver.**

There is much that can go wrong during the Communication Process: The sender (you or your marketing team) may have no idea there even is a Communication Process. The code can be wrong. The message can go out without containing the Code. The receiver can decode the message wrong. And there can be so many distractions that the receiver may not even hear the message at all.

Delivering a clear message is tricky. Think of the times you've given someone a job to do, and when you asked them to repeat it back they were so far off, you just had to shake your head.

Take a good look at the word 'Encode' in the graphic. We are going to spend a lot of time in the following chapters developing Code. That's where most marketers go wrong. They jump to creating the message without first considering the Code. But we're not going to do that. We are going to go step by step developing the code that will be the foundation for all of your promotions. To begin creating that code we will use what I call Code Sheets. The Code Sheets will make up a book called a Brand Code Playbook. In addition to having a digital Brand Code Playbook, I suggest you also make physical spiral-bound versions to keep on your desk for quick reference.

# 5

# Code Sheets

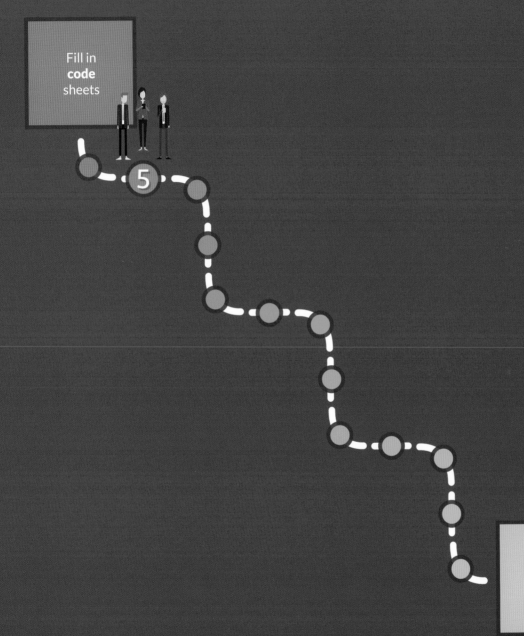

Fill in
**code**
sheets

5

Select
**channels**

# 5  Code Sheets

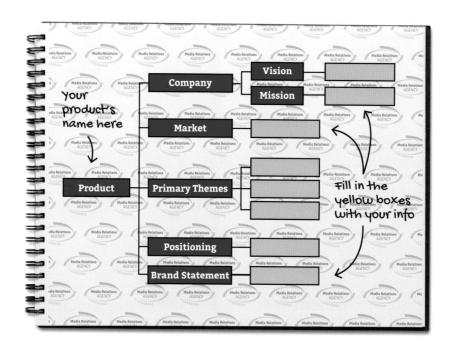

Creating Code Sheets will help you in two important ways. They are a repeatable process for documenting the code for your messages, and they will help you direct and manage your creative staff.

While Code Sheets appear simple, they will take careful thought to complete. You'll need to choose exact words for concepts that may previously have been loosely held ideas. That takes deliberation. Large companies may hold meetings to brainstorm language for this document. They may even choose to test their choices on focus groups.

You'll have one Code Sheet for your company in general, and one or more for each of your products. Each Code Sheet will be the exact same format. It's like filling out the same form over and over.

Once you have your Code Sheets completed, they will be reliable guides your team can refer to again and again. They will help in a wide variety of situations. Whether you need to create a graphic, talk to the press, give a speech or write an article, you'll have a handy guide for which points to stress. You'll have created a guidepost everyone can refer to before, during and after a project. If you consistently use your Code Sheets, your promotions will be on point no matter who works on them. Give copies of your Code Sheets to everyone involved with your promotions. Make sure they understand they are confidential and why it's important they use them.

# 6

# Institutional Promotion

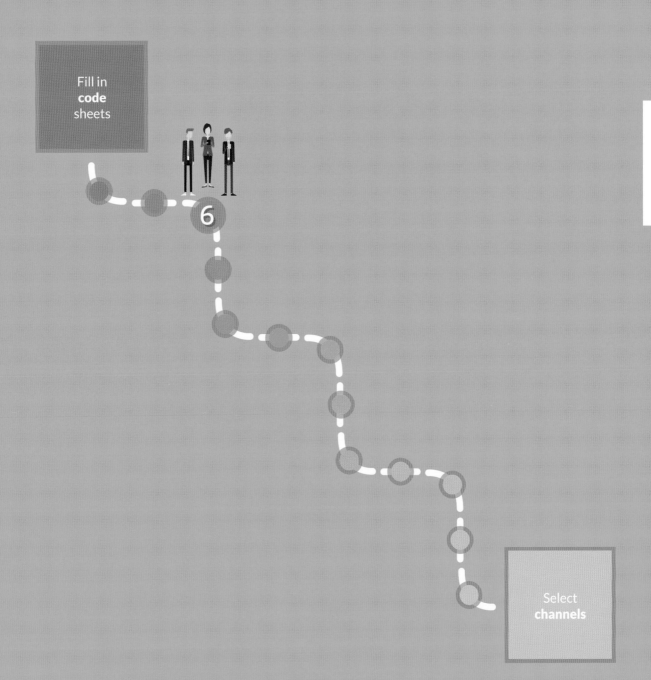

Fill in **code** sheets

6

Select **channels**

# 6 | Institutional Promotion

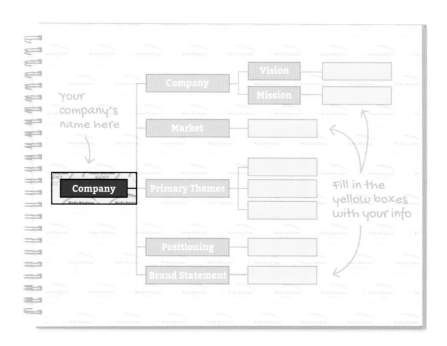

The first item you will fill out on your Code Sheet will name what you are promoting. It's easy. On the Code Sheet page for Institutional Promotion, just fill in the name of your company.

We'll discuss filling out the rest of the tabs on the Code Sheets later, but I'd like to make some comments about Institutional Promotions before we move on.
As you fill out the Code Sheet for your company, keep in mind that your Institution Promotions will have a "halo effect" on how folks view the company's individual products. Let's say a fast-food restaurant executes an Institutional Promotion initiative that speaks to the importance of keeping its kitchens sparkling clean. Those promotions will affect how customers perceive the chain's bacon cheeseburgers.

A word of caution. Never create promotions you can't live up to. Remember a Brand is built in two ways: by what you tell someone and by what they experience. If your Institutional Promotions tout sparkling clean kitchens, and someone walks in and finds the kitchen less that sparkling, they are going to develop an unfavorable Brand definition.

Despite what was just said, customers do have a tolerance for some overpromising. Especially in the food industry. Often food items pictured on menus or packaging appear far more appetizing than the actual product. It may be acceptable in some industries to overpromise and underdeliver, but it's always risky and lessens the consumer's perception no matter how slightly.

When a company creates Institutional Promotions, the promotional message is usually directed at the entire market. For example, a shoe store running institutional advertising is not likely to have separate messages for students, young families and grandparents. An ad would just direct one main message to the general public such as comfort, price or service.

In addition to acting as the code for the Institutional Promotions, this Code Sheet can also serve as a measure for the rest of your Code Sheets. You'll want to continually check back to make sure the company's other promotional undertakings are in line with its Institutional Promotion.

When a company's various forms of marketing are in sync with each other, this creates a united appeal to the customer. It helps prevent the customer from being confused or noticing conflicts in the company's message. Since repetition is necessary for branding, having a consistent theme between Institutional Promotion and individual product promotions will help consumers develop the right definition in their minds.

When a company's various forms of marketing are in sync with each other, this creates a united appeal to the customer.

# 7

# Product

Fill in **code** sheets

7

Select **channels**

# 7 Product

As mentioned, the first tab denotes what is being promoted. In the last chapter the Code Sheet began with the company. Next, you will create sheets for each individual product. If your company manufactures three products such as a boat, a boat trailer and a boat motor, each product will have its own Code Sheet (more if there are submarkets) with the name of the product listed here.

As I said, the first tab of the Code Sheet is easy. Just write in the name of whatever you are promoting.

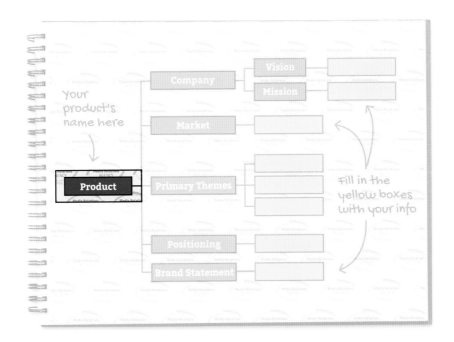

your product's name here

Fill in the yellow boxes with your info

# 8

# Vision

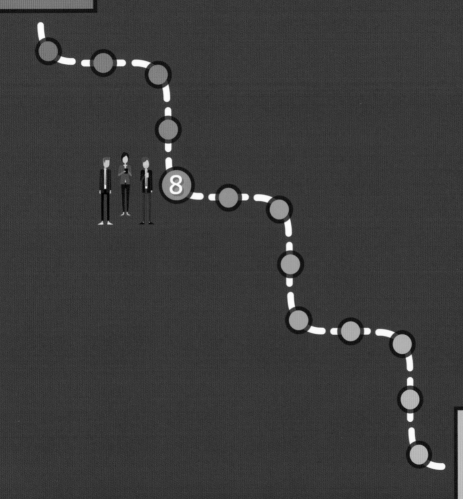

Fill in **code** sheets

Select **channels**

8

# 8 Vision

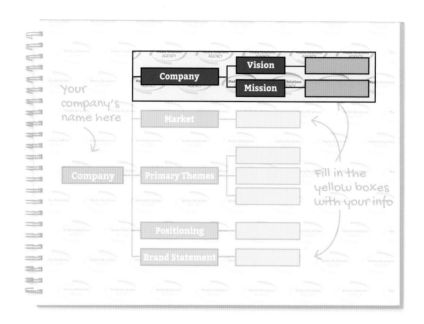

The next two chapters will discuss the Vision and Mission tabs. These two tabs are a little different than the others. Once you fill in these tabs, they will remain the same on every Code Sheet. You will fill them out once and repeat them exactly the same on every Code Sheet. Keep them short: no more than a phrase if possible. They should be easily memorized.

Let's discuss the Vision tab first and how it relates to your marketing communications.

Humans are constantly thinking. Thoughts are always moving through our minds. Once some thoughts have left our minds, they are gone forever. But some thoughts keep coming back. And the more energy we spend entertaining these thoughts, the more ingrained and powerful they become.

When a concept in your mind is strong and clear, it tends to be manifested in the physical world. Such is the case with a Company Vision.

A Company Vision is something yet to be achieved. It is an imagined state to be realized in the future. When a company founder or leader codifies the future form of the company in writing, this is a called a company Vision Statement. The leader has the responsibility of creating the vision, then communicating that vision to the rest of the company in a way it can be easily recalled.

Many times, Vision Statements are far too long for the purpose of your Code Sheets. Your Vision Statement should be short. Here's the problem with long Vision Statements. No one can remember them, and no one will take the time to repeatedly read them. Essentially, long Vision and Mission Statements are worthless. You'll need something you and the rest of your organization can keep in mind as you move through the day-to-day details of creating promotions.

If you already have a Vision Statement that is too long, and the bureaucracy of your company prevents you from shortening it, then shorten it anyway and call it your "marketing version" of the company's Vision Statement. You can always link it to the longer version in case someone needs to see it.

You might think it's impossible to come up with a Vision Statement that is only a few words, but it's not. Taking the time to distill your Vision Statement to a short, inspiring and memorable phrase might take some thinking, but it will serve your organization well.

**CODE**

8. Vision

# 9

# Mission

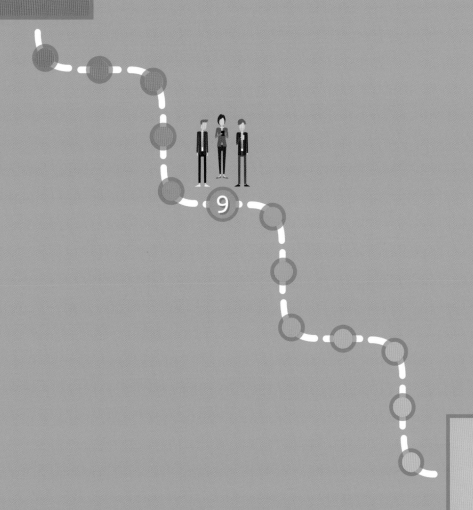

Fill in **code** sheets

9

Select **channels**

# 9 | Mission

A company Mission Statement describes how a company intends to achieve its Vision. Once again, keep it short, no more than a simple phrase. Everyone should be able to remember and repeat your mission. If it's a catchy little phrase you have a good chance that it will memorable.

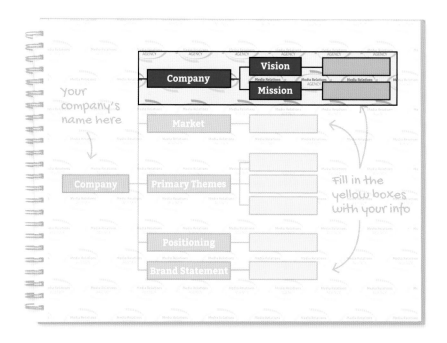

The connection between a company Vision and company Mission is this: A vision states where you are going. A mission states how you are going to get there.

For example, a pet food company's vision might be to *become the leading value pet food brand in the United States.* The mission might be to *provide flavorful and nutritious pet food at the lowest possible price.*

Having a clear Mission Statement is a reminder to your staff of how the details of the team's daily activities fit into the big picture.

A concise, usable Mission Statement contributes to morale. Having a mission confers a sense of meaning and purpose. Employees benefit from feeling like they're a part of a mission and understanding how their work fits into that mission.

As the marketing team creates promotions, have them refer to the Code Sheets to evaluate their alignment or misalignment with the company's vision and mission. Because of the creative nature of marketing promotions, it's easy to get out of alignment. Fortunately, if you use your Code Sheet to evaluate promotions before they go out, it's just as easy to make adjustments and get them back on track.

None of your marketing communications should be out of line with your company's Vision and Mission Statements. They should support them. That's the purpose of having your company Vision and Mission Statements repeated at the top of every Code Sheet page.

# 10

# Market

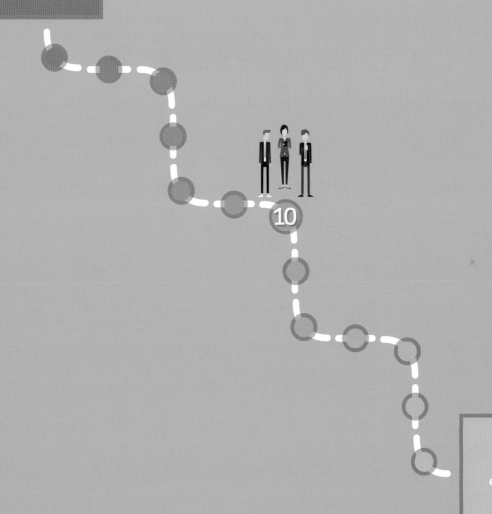

Fill in **code** sheets

10

Select **channels**

# 10 Market

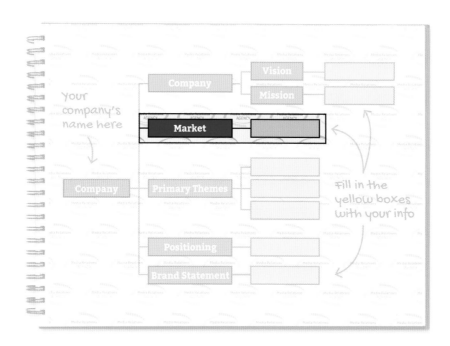

Consider the order of the Promotional Sequence from step one of the SAM 6 process: A **company** creates a **product** that it sells to a **market** using a **message** said by a **messenger** through **promotional mix** channels. Before you can create or communicate a *message*, you need to figure out who you are going to be communicating with. That's your *Market*. We will eventually get to naming your Market so you don't have to write three paragraphs to fill in this tab. But for now, let's discuss the term Market a bit.

Sometimes when overly enthusiastic CEOs are asked who should buy their product, they say everyone. But that's not true. Bald men don't need a comb, skinny people don't need a weight-loss pill, and preschoolers don't need a beer while they watch the Superbowl.

Your Market is always a subset of humans on planet Earth. It includes anyone who has the need and means to purchase your product or to influence the purchase of your product.

Your Market, at some point, must have the need or at least the desire to purchase your product. In addition, to be included in your Market a person must have access to the money for purchasing the product. Most people would love to have a private jet but few have enough money to purchase one. However, it is possible that someone would not have money to purchase your product yet still be considered part of your Market. Those people are called influencers. Young children may not have money, but they are powerful influencers.

Women can also be influencers when it comes to men's health care. It's women who make most of the health care decisions for their husbands and the phenomenon even has a name: "woman to man". Adult children of elderly parents is another example of influencer vs. purchaser dynamics.

There are a few things to consider about your Market such as building out a Market Profile (that's where we will come up with a name for your Market) and selecting a Market Segmentation Strategy. These will be addressed in the next two chapters. First is Market Segmentation.

Your market is always a subset of humans on planet Earth. It includes anyone who has the need and means to purchase your product or to influence the purchase of your product.

# 11

# Market Segmentation Strategy

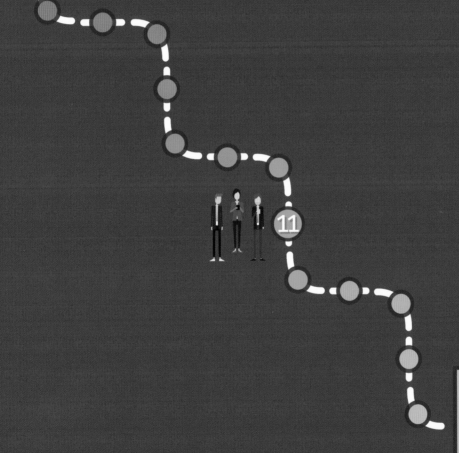

Fill in **code** sheets

11

Select **channels**

# 11 Market Segmentation Strategy

Markets can be divided into segments with similar characteristics. These market segments are called submarkets. But how many submarkets should your market be divided into? Three? Eight? Fifty? None at all? There are four Segmentation Strategies that will help you answer that question: **Undifferentiated, Concentrated, Multi-Segmented and Micro-Segmented.**

Should you segment your market? Sometimes, but not always.

It's easy to get enamored with Market Segmentation. But before you get swept up in the excitement of segmenting your market, remember that the more submarkets you have, the more time and manpower it will take to reach them. You can easily quadruple your cost and workload by segmenting one market into four.

A good rule of thumb is don't segment a market unless you have to.

With that said, there are times it makes good sense to segment. Let's look at four Segmentation Strategies.

**Undifferentiated targeting strategy**

Using one promotional strategy for the entire market

**Concentrated targeting strategy**

Tailoring promotions only to the most lucrative market segment

**Multi-segmented targeting strategy**

Creating unique promotions to multiple market segments

**Micro-segmented targeting strategy**

Marketing to the individual person

# Undifferentiated – 1

The Undifferentiated strategy means that there is no Market Segmentation. The entire market is treated as one group. Using an Undifferentiated strategy, everyone in your market gets the same message. Your promotions treat your entire market as one persona.

# Concentrated – 1, 2 or 3

With a Concentrated segmentation strategy, you isolate one, two or three primary market segments that have the most potential value. For example, if you are selling futons, you may notice there are four distinct groups that purchase futons: college students, young professionals, parents and retirees. But you also notice that two groups, college students and young professionals, purchase the most futons. So you allocate your resources to promotions aimed at those two submarkets.

You know that parents and retirees purchase futons too, but at a much lesser rate. Rather than market to them, it's better to use your limited resources on the more lucrative markets.

Keep in mind that all promotions have a halo effect. While you might not be promoting futons directly to parents and retirees, they may still see your promotions and be persuaded to purchase.

## Multi-segmented – 4+

A Multi-Segmented strategy creates separate marketing messages for four or more different market segments. For example, a mall developer who is planning the opening of a new shopping center may want to attract so many people to this opening that it runs separate marketing campaigns for children, teenagers, young professionals, parents, tourists and retirees.

## Micro-segmented – individual

A Micro-Segmented strategy targets marketing all the way down to the individual level. For instance, online retailers may keep track of enough information about individual shoppers to be able to suggest specific products suited to an individual shopper's personal tastes.

# With segmenting comes complexity

If you decide that you need to segment your market, it will take more discipline to carry out your plan. For example, if you sell fine handmade suits and decide that your advertising budget is best spent on a Concentrated strategy geared to both wealthy executives and entry-level professionals hoping to make an impression, you'll have a challenge on your hands. When designing your website, wealthy executives may not like being seen in suits associated with wet-behind-the-ears newcomers.

Even more complicated would be a Multi-Segmented strategy where your suits are right for business, weddings, funerals, formal dinner parties and casual get-togethers. Your website may end up looking as though it has multiple personalities. Site visitors from any one submarket might be confused and feel they have come to the wrong place for their needs.

The most common use of segmentation strategies I've seen over the last 40 years, and the one you will likely adopt, is to implement an Undifferentiated strategy when promoting the company in general, and a Concentrated strategy when promoting products. It is usually the case that most of the sales come from just a couple submarkets. If you adopt the attitude of "no sale left behind", be prepared to spend heavily on smaller, low-producing submarkets.

Large companies often adopt a Multi-Segmented or even Micro-Segmented strategy. They have the money and manpower to squeeze juice from small, relatively unproductive submarkets. Another reason they might chase after small submarkets is to protect against a competitor getting a foothold. A large company might rather forfeit profit capturing a tiny segment of the market than relinquish it to a competitor.

My advice to most companies is don't confuse the *ability* to segment with whether you *should* segment. The access to profiling information that data compilers give us today can be very useful but it can also seduce you into chasing unprofitable submarkets. Remember my earlier advice: A good rule of thumb is don't segment a market unless you have to.

# 12

# Market Profile

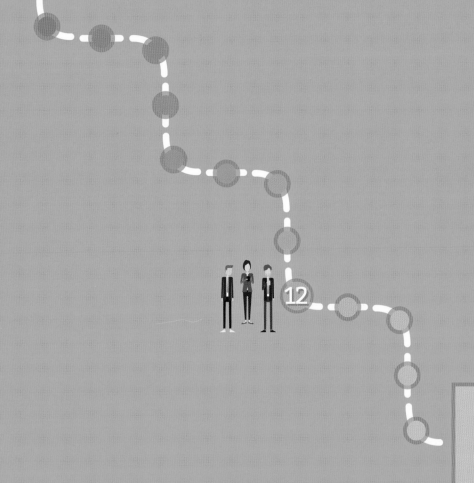

Fill in **code** sheets

12

Select **channels**

# 12 Market Profile

As mentioned earlier, segmenting markets leads to more work. If your product needs to be divided into submarkets, you will create a separate Code Sheet for each one. In other words, if you have three products and each product has three submarkets, you will have nine Code Sheets. Ten if you count the one for Institutional Promotion.

When you segment your market, you are building profiles of like groups of people. There are countless variables that can be used when segmenting your market. Segmentation variables can be literally any characteristic that makes one group different from another. As an extreme example, a submarket could consist of blonde men between the ages of 30 and 40 who have won a spelling bee, own a red Chevy, love to eat olives and have mothers named Kathy.

A submarket could also be constructed of just two general variables: all females between ages 20 and 30.

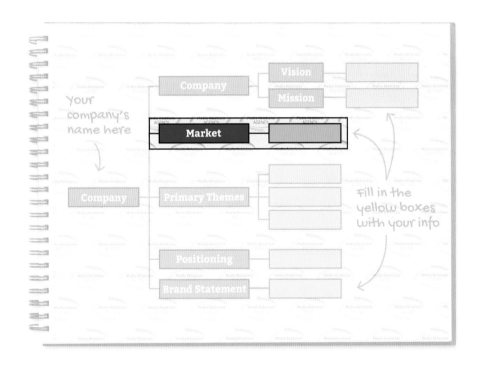

There are categories of segmentation variables which are useful for building a profile. They are:

## Demographics

Characteristics such as gender, age, family life cycle and income.

## Psychographics

How people think, such as rock musicians thinking differently than librarians.

## Geographics

Where people live, such as downtown in a big city or on a farm on the prairie.

## Benefits Sought

The reasons why people buy products, such as whether someone bought a new phone because they really needed the features or because they thought it would be fun to own the latest technology.

## Usage Rate

How much someone consumes a product, such as whether they drink cola constantly throughout the day or only have it as an occasional treat.

Creating a market or submarket Profile (persona) is like starting with a stick person and continually building out a character profile. By the time you are done building a Profile of your submarket, it can be hard to hold all those variables in your mind. Here are some fun tactics that will be helpful.

Most submarkets fall within a certain age range. Let's say that range is 35 to 45 with the mid-age being 40. You can name your submarket by finding the most popular baby names 40 years ago. Assuming the year is 1978, you'll find Jason and Jennifer were at, or very near, the top of the list.

Many submarkets are weighted toward one gender or the other. For our example, a submarket may be 70% female and 30% male. In this case you would put the dominate gender name first as a nod to the larger group. So you would refer to your submarket as Jennifer and Jason rather than Jason and Jennifer.

Taking this one step further, assume that your market is split between two socioeconomic classes: one with advanced degrees and high incomes, and one with high school degrees and limited incomes. You can give the upper class market the more formal names of Jennifer and Jason. And give the other market the shortened nicknames of Jen and Jas.

Just as hearing a friend's name can immediately conjure up their persona, hearing a well-defined submarket's name can have the same effect.

Now imagine you are in a marketing meeting, and the boss comes in and says we need to raise our prices. You might say, "I think raising prices for Jennifer and Jason is a good idea but I think we might lose customers with Jen and Jas. I just can't see Jen and Jas paying more. Maybe we need to keep the price the same for Jen and Jas, and scale back the features of the product a little to keep the price down."

Building profiles of your submarkets and naming them brings them to life. At Media Relations Agency, we talk about our two submarkets like they are old friends. It's not unusual for me to overhear someone saying something like, "I think that's fine for Kevin and Pam but not Larry and Carol." I know just what they are talking about.

Naming your submarkets also helps keep the description of your market on the Code Sheets short. It's my opinion that if Code Sheets aren't kept to one brief page, the average employee won't use them.

# 13

# Full Value Proposition

Fill in **code** sheets

13

Select **channels**

# 13 Full Value Proposition

Once you have chosen a product, established your market segmentation strategy, and built profiles of your market and any submarkets you will be targeting, it's time to create an all-encompassing list of reasons why each group buys. You'll do this by creating a Full Value Proposition. The Value Points on the list you create will help you fill in the Primary Theme boxes on your code sheets.

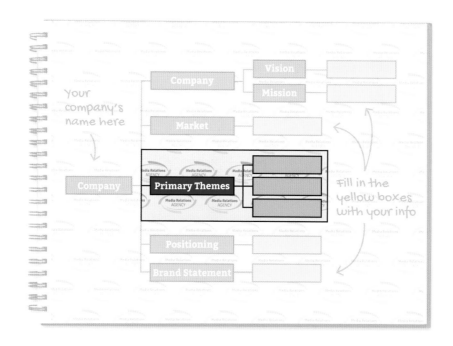

There are often many reasons people purchase a product. One person might buy a bag of oranges because the quantity fits their need. Another may buy a bag of oranges from Florida simply because they had a nice vacation there. Another might like the shade of color and yet another might purchase oranges because they are the most expensive, and therefore assume they will be the best tasting.

Creating a Full Value Proposition is the process of assembling a comprehensive list of as many reasons a customer might buy as you can think of. There are lots of ways of going about this. You and your marketing team could just sit in a room and think them up. You could use the internet to do secondary research. Or you can spend into this by doing primary market research using focus groups or utilizing surveys.

This is what a partial list for a bag of oranges might look like:

**Full Value Proposition**
**for** oranges

- Low cost
- High quality
- Flavor
- Rich orange color
- See-through packaging
- Convenient handle on the bag
- Nice texture
- Firm
- Thick skin
- Nice logo
- Label on each orange
- Nice scent
- Cloth net package feels nice
- High in vitamin C
- Can make fresh juice
- Convenient to pack in a lunch
- Good for you

In a previous chapter we referred to the Communication Process and said the Code Sheets will help you develop the code for your message. The Full Value Proposition is an important part of that code.

After this extensive list of reasons the customer buys has been established, we'll take our Full Value Proposition a step further and divide it into two categories: Primary Value Points and Secondary Value Points.

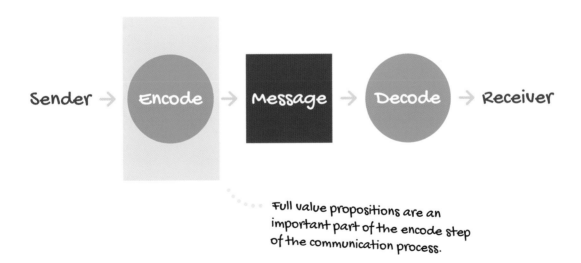

Sender → Encode → Message → Decode → Receiver

Full value propositions are an important part of the encode step of the communication process.

# 14

# Primary Value Points

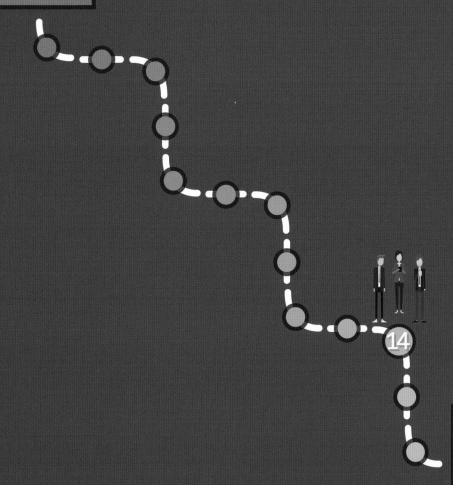

Fill in **code** sheets

Select **channels**

14

# 14 Primary Value Points

(Listed as Primary *Message Themes* on the Code Sheet)

Not all value points in your Full Value Proposition list are of equal importance. With most products, you will find there are one, two or three main reasons most people purchase a product. These main reasons are called Primary Value Points.

For instance, someone vacationing might choose to stay overnight at a hotel primarily because it is located on the beach and also because it has a nice workout facility. But the fact that the hotel is located on the beach is the primary reason for choosing the hotel. It helps that the hotel has a nice fitness center, but the fitness center is not the main reason for choosing the hotel.

You will need to determine which Value Points from your Full Value Proposition are the most important to your market.

Once you have determined your top Value Points (one, two, three, maybe four), you will rank them in order of priority. Often there is one main reason people buy and a couple other significant reasons. Prioritizing the top Value Points will help in a later step of the SAM 6 process when we plan the frequency of your messages.

Remember, if you've identified submarkets for that product, you will have separate Code Sheets and you will need to figure out the Primary Value Points for each submarket. Using the hotel as an example, one submarket might be vacationers and another might be business travelers. A person traveling for business might choose the hotel because it is close to nearby businesses they plan to visit and because the hotel offers free continental breakfast. The vacationer will likely choose the hotel for its proximity to the beach.

If you notice that the Primary Value Points are the same for multiple submarkets, that's a good indication you did not need to segment that market.

Your Primary Value Points will be listed in order of priority on your Code Sheets.

Secondary Value Points are treated differently than Primary Value Points. In most cases, they don't need to be prioritized. They are a bulleted list that is used to support the story of the Primary Value Points.

Think of your Primary Value Points as starring actors in your product's story. The Secondary Value Points are the supporting actors. They show up in the story from time to time. Without them, the story wouldn't be as interesting. Be careful though. If you get too many supporting actors in a story, the audience can get confused and become sidetracked from the main points.

Your story might even open with a Secondary Value Point, just as a movie might open with a supporting actor. For example, imagine a movie where the first scene is a man in a trenchcoat having coffee at the counter in a diner. He reads the paper, chats with the waitress and then steps out into the street. A car follows suspiciously behind as he begins walking. He notices and begins to run. The car speeds up. Its window opens. A gun flashes. The supporting actor falls dead, never to appear in the movie again.

Now, with that analogy in mind, imagine a television commercial for a luxury car. The first shot is a close up of what appears to be the rectangular dial of an expensive wristwatch. The time is five a.m. The camera slowly pans out to show you are actually looking at the stylish design of a clock centered in the dashboard of a car. The camera continues to pan back showing the rich leather interior. Then right through the back window and now you are seeing the sleek look of the rear of the car. The camera pans wider and now the clock has disappeared into the background. Now you see a well-dressed woman with a briefcase and a cup of coffee leaving a luxurious home in an upscale neighborhood walking to the car. The commercial has led with a Secondary Value Point (the stylish clock) then moved on to the Primary Value Points of the stylish interior, the stylish exterior, and finally the spoils of the early riser that signify the upscale lifestyle the car represents.

Whether you support your story with Secondary Value Points or lead with them, the promotion should always circle back to one or more of your Primary Value Points. Because that's why most people buy.

Here's a little twist. Rather than using the term Primary Value Points on the Code Sheets, the term Primary *Themes* is used. You want to be careful that the people crafting your promotions don't get tripped up by the word *Point*. Communication is not about simply repeating points. It's about telling stories. When you use the term Primary *Themes*, it's a signal to your creative team to use their imaginations. Through both words and pictures, there are countless ways to tell a story that reiterates the same point.

Thinking of your Primary Value Points as themes adds variety which makes promotions interesting, while always staying on point.

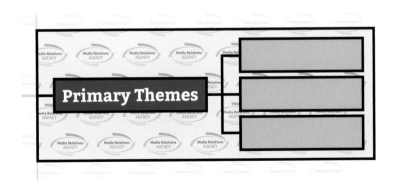

# 15

# Positioning

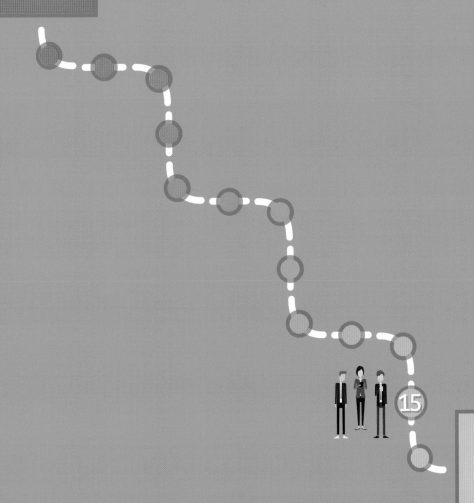

Fill in **code** sheets

Select **channels**

15

# 15 Positioning

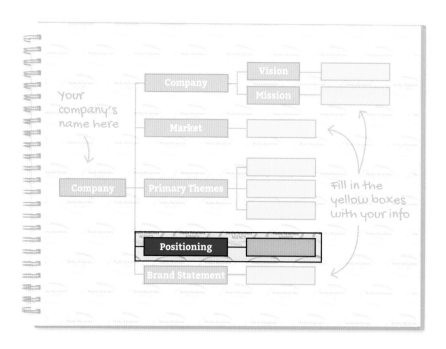

Positioning is defined as how your product is positioned in the mind of the consumer compared to the competition.

Wouldn't it be nice if your product was the only one on the market? Unfortunately, your product doesn't exist in a vacuum. Consumers are used to having many options to fill whatever need arises. As a marketer, you have to be aware of the options consumers have.

Positioning is an important part of branding. Pointing out how your product is different than the competitor's product shapes the consumers' thinking and therefore your brand. Initially, you might be reluctant to point out your competitor's weaknesses. However, marketing is serious business, it's not social correspondence. There are competitors who would love to have your customers.

Some factors that may be a part of your product's Positioning include price, quality, speed of delivery, convenience, etc.

One reason there are competing products is that no product can meet every need every consumer has. For example, a new home cannot simultaneously be ultra-luxurious and low-cost. Many times, consumers will be looking for a product with certain Positioning. For example, if a customer needs shoes to wear during a home renovation product, she may be specifically looking for tennis shoes that are durable enough to protect her feet from debris but also cheap enough to discard if they get covered with paint. The customer may just want a generic, affordable pair of tennis shoes that have utility value. They do not need to be on-trend. If a shoe manufacturer wants to position itself in this portion of the market, the manufacturer will want to keep costs down and not spend extra money adapting to short-lived style fads.

Positioning relates closely to step 3 in the Consumer Buying Process—one of the 31 terms in the back of this book.

The Consumer Buying process goes like this:

① A person recognizes that they have a need.

② They start to think about it and look for information that will help them with their decision.

③ **They compare products and narrow them down to the ones that best meet their need.**

④ They make their purchase

⑤ Finally, after the purchase, they consider if they made the right decision.

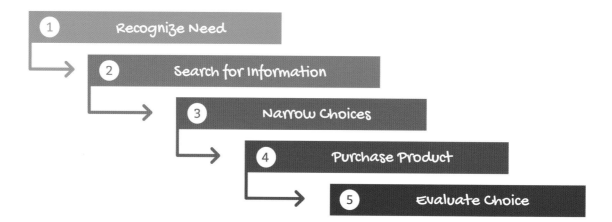

When a customer is about to choose between your product and the competition's, it needs to be clear in their mind why yours is a better choice.

If the purchase is an inexpensive product like a candy bar or half-gallon of milk, the Consumer Buying Process can happen in a matter of seconds. For big-ticket items such as a car or a home, the process may take weeks, months or even years.

Here is how the Consumer Buying Process aligns with the purchase of a vehicle:

1. This car is getting old.

2. I think I'll stop by a couple dealerships this weekend and see what they have.

3. Wow, I really like the style of the new Suburbans but the Tahoe gets better gas mileage.

4. I'm buying the Suburban.

5. Now that I'm at the gas station filling up my new Suburban, I wish I had gotten the Tahoe because of the better gas mileage.

**Be bold when expressing why your product is better than the competition.**

In addition to the Primary Message Themes, Positioning is an important part of building your brand. Don't be afraid to speak with conviction. If your product is better than product x and y, tell the consumer in no uncertain terms, "No one can match our low, low price because we buy in volume that's unheard of in our industry." Or, "There's a reason you pay more for our widget than widget x and y. Our widget is made with parts that don't break after six months. Under normal wear and tear, our parts last 25 years or longer. You'd have to buy 50 of theirs for every one of ours."

Marketing is a little like politics–you don't want to wait for your opponent to define you. And if your competition is asleep at the wheel, you might want to "help" them along with their definition.

How many times have you been talking about something you are thinking of buying and heard someone say, "Ya, but I read somewhere that bla, bla, bla." It's a good bet the competition had a hand in casting seeds of doubt.

I'm not advocating you make up facts or distort your competition's weakness. I'm just telling you that for marketing and branding purposes, make sure you point out why your product is better for your market than the other choices they will surely be considering.

Positioning helps tip the scales
in your favor when consumers
compare products.

# Brand Statement

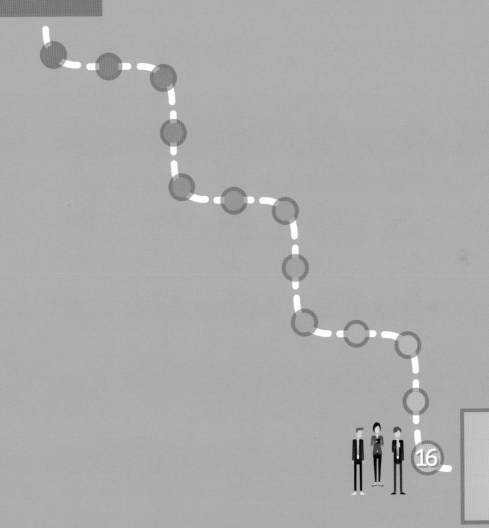

Fill in **code** sheets

16

Select **channels**

# 16 | Brand Statement

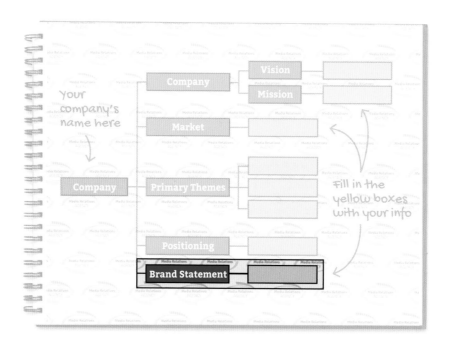

The last tab on your Code Sheet is another marketing concept I thought up several years ago as I was mulling over the term Brand. It occurred to me that if the correct definition of Brand is *the definition people hold in their minds of a company and its products*, it would make sense to imagine what that definition would sound like and write it down. The name I came up with for this concept was Brand Statement.

After a couple years of using Brand Statement inhouse, I thought to Google it to see if the term Brand Statement might already be in use. Sure enough, it was. However, my concept of Brand Statement is different than the ones you will find on the internet. Think of a Brand Statement as the bullseye all marketing communications are aiming for. Your Brand Statement is written in the voice of a customer and consists of your *Primary Messages* and your *Positioning*. It's an ideal definition consumers hold in their minds as it would be said out loud.

Here's how to write a Brand Statement. Imagine you are sitting in a coffee shop and you overhear the two people at the next table. One person is explaining your company, or one of your products, to the other and they get it exactly right. Their words come out just how you would want to hear them and you are thrilled. That's your Brand Statement.

Your Brand Statement is when one person is explaining your company or one of your products to the other and they get it exactly right.

Write your Brand Statement in plain language just as someone might actually say it. For instance, let's say Home Depot's Primary Value Points were: 1. *Wide product mix,* 2. *Friendly staff.* 3. *Low prices.* And its positioning was *more do-it-yourself classes.*

If someone was branded correctly and described Home Depot to a friend, the Brand Statement might sound like this: "Home Depot is where I always go for home improvement projects. It seems like they have everything I need no matter what it is. And the people who work there are so darn friendly. I don't know how they keep their prices so low with such good service, but I'm glad they do. And the best part is all the do-it-yourself classes they offer. I'm becoming a bit of a DIY expert. I just love shopping there. I wouldn't go anywhere else."

Did you notice the casual, conversational language? The definition you create in your market's minds will contain the essence of your code but it won't be bullet points. People don't think or speak in bullet points. Writing a Brand Statement for the Code Sheets this way helps the people who are tasked with creating and delivering your message see the bridge from your code to the actual definition or Brand. This way, a writer, spokesperson or artist can say, "Ok, I get where you're going. I can get people to think that way."

The previous example was for a company. Here's an example of a Brand Statement for a product. "Hey, I heard about this new hand lotion, Seaka, that you only have to put on once and it works all day. It even keeps working after you wash your hands. It's more expensive than other lotions but hey, I deserve a little luxury. A story I read in a magazine said they use a certain type of seagrass as an ingredient which makes it smell really nice. I'm going to order some online and give it a try."

## How to use a Brand Statement

A Brand Statement is a prototype of your Brand. A lifelike model of the real thing that gives your creative team clear direction of what you want them to accomplish. You are telling them very clearly, this is how I want people to think when you are finished creating the mailing, brochure, website content or whatever it is they are creating.

As a manager, you can also use your Brand Statement as a litmus test before the communication goes out. It's a helpful tool for making sure your promotions are supporting the definition you want your customers to end up with.

## Easy as pie?

If this is all sounding a little too easy, it's not. Even under the best conditions, say a classroom full of adult learners who are eager and paying attention, it's still difficult to get everyone thinking and saying the same thing. Each individual person has unique experiences and preconceived opinions. You can't totally control what people think. But *you can* control your messaging. If you keep your message focused and repeated across all promotional channels, people will pick up on your message. And people will generally retain the definition you're trying to form in their minds.

You may notice that after writing your Primary Message Themes and Positioning in the form of a Brand Statement that it doesn't sound quite right. That means there's something wrong with your Primary Message Themes or Positioning. Maybe you've forgotten to include something, or realize a Secondary Value Point is actually a primary one. If this happens, go back and make the appropriate change to your Code Sheet.

You may find you want to modify your Code Sheet to include more fields. That's fine. Maybe you want to add a field that addresses why customers *don't* but *should* buy from you or you want to highlight your Unique Selling Proposition. Feel free to modify the form if you need to. But a word of caution. Resist the temptation to get wordy and complex. This is Code, not the message.

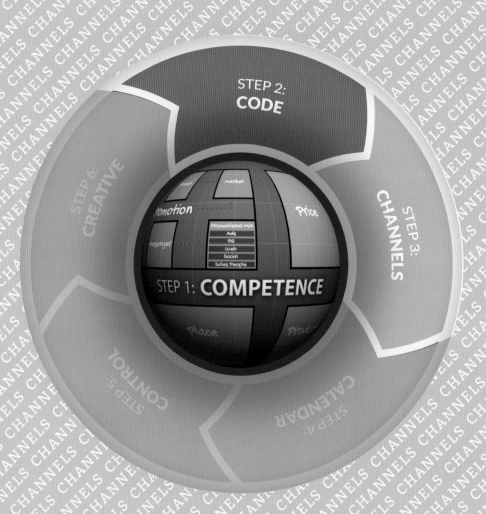

STEP 2:
**CODE**

STEP 3: **CHANNELS**

STEP 6: **CREATIVE**

STEP 5: **CONTROL**

STEP 4: **CALENDAR**

Market

Promotion

Price

Messenger

Promotional Mix
Ads
PR
Web
Social
Sales People

Place

Product

STEP 1: **COMPETENCE**

# CHANNELS

Let's decide which promotional mix channels will give us the best return.

I wonder which channels reach our market the best?

We need to use channels that give us enough space to tell a persuasive story.

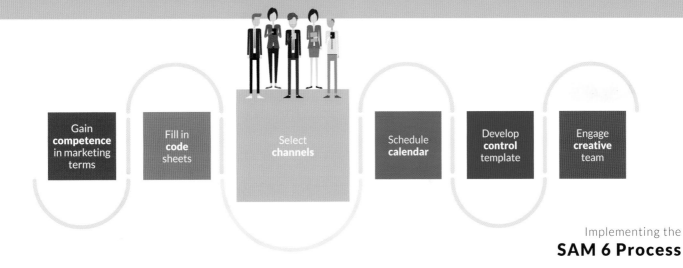

Gain **competence** in marketing terms

Fill in **code** sheets

Select **channels**

Schedule **calendar**

Develop **control** template

Engage **creative** team

Implementing the
**SAM 6 Process**

# 17

# Promotional Mix

Select
**channels**

17

Schedule
**calendar**

# 17 Promotional Mix

(Not to be confused with the *Marketing* Mix)

In step 2, part of the Code Sheet is identifying the people you are trying to reach, your market. So where are these people hanging out during the day and what are they doing? Are they driving? Are they online? At home? At work? Are they listening to the radio? On Facebook? Reading trade journals?

You'll need to think about those questions in relation to how you can reach them with your message.

You can promote your product in countless ways such as bus benches, commercials on TV, events, media stories and with brochures. You could even put a sandwich board on your dog and take it for a walk in the city. Fortunately, all of the millions of ways in which you can communicate with your market can be categorized into a few main channels called the Promotional Mix. If you search the internet and textbooks, you will find a variety of combinations of promotional channel mixes ranging in quantity from four to maybe ten or twelve.

The Promotional Mix is most often categorized as Advertising, Publicity, Personal Selling and Sales Promotions. There are two drawbacks to that set of categories. The category *Sales Promotions*, which is coupons, sweepstakes, rebate programs, etc., is more a tactic than a communication channel. That mix also doesn't call out the internet as a separate channel.

At the other end of the spectrum you will find the Promotional Mix categorized in long lists that include direct market advertising, events, product placement in movies, etc. The drawback of having too many categories is that you can't hold them neatly in your mind. In my opinion, it unnecessarily over-complicates the Promotional Mix.

The Promotional Mix I've settled on for Media Relations Agency, and the one I recommend for you, consists of media coverage, website, social media, advertising and personal selling. This categorization of the Promotional Mix is self-descriptive and easy to remember.

Whatever combination of Promotional Mix categories you decide fits your need, the purpose remains the same: organizing and prioritizing the use of the Promotional Mix to get the best results you can, from the money and manpower you have.

How you allocate your resources into the different channels depends on a variety of factors. Each channel has pros and cons, such as *bandwidth*, the length of time or space to deliver the message; *control*, your influence in delivering the message; *believability*, how likely a consumer is to trust the information; *reach*, how widely the message is delivered; and *price*, the expense in time and dollars to deliver the message.

Let's discuss some pros and cons for each Promotional Mix channel in more detail. At the end of this chapter you will see them organized in a table as a quick guide to aid in selecting the most productive Promotional Mix channels.

## Media coverage

Media coverage, also referred to as publicity, is a powerful Promotional Mix channel. I know a little bit about this channel because our agency has inserted tens of thousands of media stories into living rooms (and bathrooms too for those of you who take your news on the toilet) all across North America. The power of publicity is best understood at 40,000 feet. Next time you fly on a clear night, look down and imagine your product's story streaming into homes in every city. No one has the ear of the public like the media.

Media coverage has many pros and a few cons. First, the pros. Nothing will outsell good media coverage. Its massive audiences and storytelling format are two big pluses. The facts that people are actively listening and it's inexpensive are a couple more. Add to that the bragging rights and the distinct possibility that most of your competitors aren't getting much coverage, and you have arguably the most powerful promotional channel on the planet.

I could go on and on about the benefits of publicity like it being a third-party endorsement, how great it is when other people say nice things about you, and how it can be reused in other promotions for years.

It's always surprising how few companies (and more surprisingly PR firms) have figured out how to get a substantial amount of media coverage for their company and products. It's almost a given when you study the history of cash cow brands that you find media coverage played an integral role in their success.

Media coverage does have some cons. You can't schedule it, and you don't have absolute control over the message. But big deal. Common sense will tell you, if a media story were to run tomorrow about your product, you'd see a boost in sales. And if stories about your product were popping up in key markets all year long, it would surely impact year-end numbers.

I should also point out that our terrific success with media coverage is largely due to the fact that we've removed one of publicity's disadvantages. Most PR firms charge a fee whether or not they actually secure any media coverage. That means they have your money and you don't, no matter their success. But not us. We remove that risk by charging per story we arrange. Our nationally trademarked Pay Per Interview Publicity® pricing model assures clients always get publicity for their money. Our clients love the accountability and it shows in our sales.

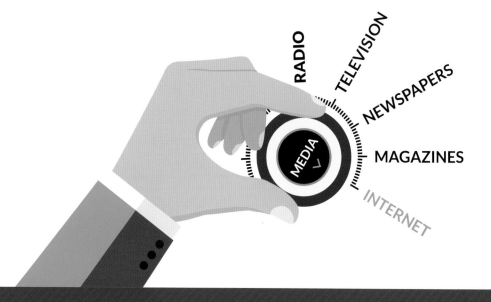

The launch of Breathe Right Nasal Strips is one of our many media coverage success stories. Most people mistakenly think Breathe Right's success began with the endorsement of football star Jerry Rice. That's not the case. It began with Media Relations Agency arranging a two-year stream of media interviews for Dr. Cohen introducing his new product to the world. I don't want to get sidetracked with a long story but if you want, you can go the blog on our website publicity.com, search for "the Breathe Right story," and read about it in detail. It's pretty interesting.

## Websites

Websites are the most dynamic channel of the Promotional Mix. They can be as simple as a brochure, or as complex as an online store, and everything in between.

Websites have many strong points. They provide plenty of bandwidth to tell your story. You own your site, so you can say as much as you want. You also control it, so you can say exactly *what* you want. You get to tell your story precisely how you wish, limited only by creativity and technical skill.

Another positive attribute to websites is their low cost. In many cases you'll pay less for a website that's available globally than you would to rent a single billboard. But there's a catch: You need to use other promotions to drive traffic to your website, and that can get expensive. Without additional marketing, even the best-designed website will not have much reach.

Another drawback to websites is that consumers are well aware of where the content comes from. Consumers are savvy. They know you've created or chosen your own website content. They know your website is a sales message. But while they may not completely trust everything they see on your site, they won't disregard it, either. You can build credibility by using tactics such as testimonials and posting favorable media coverage. When web visitors see media clips or articles featuring your product, they know a third party found your product noteworthy.

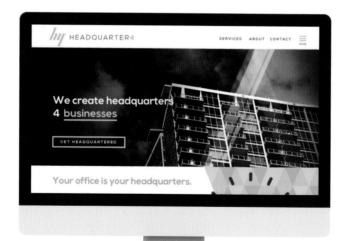

Think of your website as an opportunity to tell your product's story.

# Social Media

There are many reasons marketers pour so much time and energy into social media. Social media is fun, it's personal, it's engaging and it's interactive. Not only that, it lets you develop trust and build relationships with consumers, as well as field customer comments and discover what they really think about your products. With social media, you can send short messages on Facebook and Twitter, and develop your ideas further in a blog. You can post messages on social media networks that millions of people can access, and you can deliver your message on a blog your company controls completely. There are so many interesting possibilities with this promotional channel that it can be overwhelming.

Yet, just as social media seems to have infinite possibilities, it also may seem like it's causing infinite work. At first, embarking on several social media channels can seem exciting. But once you start posting on a social media site or on your blog, you realize you're running on a treadmill that moves fast and never shuts down. You need to constantly keep posting, posting, posting. Not because you are necessarily struck with inspiration, but because you can't let your content go stale. If people see that you haven't posted to Facebook in a few months or that your last blog entry is from a year ago, they may wonder what you have been doing in the meantime. They may wonder if you don't follow through with projects or if you forget about things. Keeping your social media content fresh can be like trying to keep your house clean or quench your thirst with salt water. It's never ending.

And you can't post just anything. You shouldn't, anyway. Your content needs to have quality and depth to it. It can't just be cheerful observations with a lot of exclamation points. It has to have value. It needs to provide your audience with information that's worth their time. And it needs to be well written. That's not an easy thing these days. People who were raised with technology may be very good at learning new tools, but they may also have had their writing polluted by text message acronyms, IMO. Good writing takes not only education but experience and artfulness. It takes time to create. And it's so subjective that your people may all have different opinions about what's good enough.

Does that mean you shouldn't do it? No. If your potential customers are reading it, write away. Personal writing in a social media post helps personalize your company. It shows that your corporation is made up of real people. It can help consumers get to know you on an individual level. But be aware that figuring out social media marketing is like shaking hands with an octopus. Sometimes you're not really sure what to do with all those arms.

## Advertising

Advertising is often the first approach that comes to mind when people think of marketing. Advertising can be thought of in two categories: traditional and digital. Let's talk about traditional ads first.

Traditional advertising offers some nice advantages over digital ads. For one thing, you don't need to worry about technical considerations such as keywords and phrases needed for search engine optimization. Traditional ads are also a good way to reach older audiences.

My parents are in their eighties and while they have computers, printers and cell phones, they are not comfortable with them. Their generation grew into adulthood reading the newspaper, watching television, reading magazines and listening to the radio. And guess what? That's what they still do. It's like technology migrated into their home, but they didn't migrate to the technology. If you are selling hearing aids or reverse mortgages, it's a good bet you can still reach your market through old-school ads.

A drawback to traditional advertising is that it's expensive. You'll pay a handsome sum for print or TV ads, especially if you want to reach large audiences. And consumers may not even notice them. It's easy to skip, ignore or flip right past ads. The cost of advertising also puts a crimp in the amount of time or space you'll have to get your message across.

Digital ads, on the other hand, have their own set of advantages and disadvantages. What's great about digital ads is that they are inexpensive and highly targeted. You can send them to such a specific audience that it's almost scary. And you can track their success in great detail. But they can easily fall prey to consumer distaste: Consumers may ignore digital ads or even use ad-blocking techniques to avoid seeing them altogether. And digital ads don't provide space for detailed product explanations or persuasive arguments. Digital ads are like short reminders or taglines. In terms of introducing your audience to a product, they're more like a thumbprint than a handshake.

Despite their cons, digital ads have some nice advantages. A big one is scalability. If you hit on a winning ad you can quickly expand its reach. Testing multiple taglines and graphics is also inexpensive. The low cost of experimentation is a real plus.

## Personal Selling

Ah, the good old-fashioned salesperson. Nothing will ever replace a personal relationship. A person who can laugh at your jokes, tell a story and sympathize with your concerns can be far more convincing than the most beautiful magazine ad. Yet the effectiveness of personal selling is almost completely dependent on the person you employ. While a likeable, motivated salesperson can sell a tremendous amount of product, most can't. Some are abrasive and off-putting. Others just don't have the heart for it. Good salespeople are few and far between.

Salespeople also have a relatively small reach. The most hardworking rep can only talk to a fraction of the people that one media story could reach. And personal selling is expensive. Salespeople have mortgages to pay. Digital ads don't. Because of personal selling's low reach and high expense, use personal selling for high-ticket items where the product is complex and a relationship is required.

## Analyzing the Promotional Mix Channels

There are many variables to consider when deciding on the right mix of promotional channels for promoting your company and its products. Organizing the channels and variables into a table will help you evaluate each channel's advantages and disadvantages. Looking at the Promotional Mix channels in this way can help you choose the ones that are the best fit for reaching your audience, explaining your product, and getting the most bang out of your budget and manpower.

Every company and product is different and may require a different Promotional Mix for optimal results. The rows of channels and columns of variables can be as delineated as necessary. For instance, you could have just one row that says social media, or you could have multiple rows for social media that list Facebook, Twitter, LinkedIn, Google+ and Pinterest. It's up to you.

Here's a what a simple generalized table looks like to get you started.

| | Cost Effective | Mass Marketing | Long Message | Market Listening | Quick Time Frame | Control of Message | $ | $$ | $$$ |
|---|---|---|---|---|---|---|---|---|---|
| **Publicity** | | | | | | | | | |
| Main Channels: | | | | | | | | | |
| 1) | | | | | | | | | |
| 2) | | | | | | | | | |
| 3) | | | | | | | | | |
| Secondary Channels: | | | | | | | | | |

**Publicity**

- Newspaper
- Magazine
- TV
- Radio
- Digital

| | | | | | | | | | |
|---|---|---|---|---|---|---|---|---|---|
| Main Channels: | | | | | | | | | |
| 1) | | | | | | | | | |
| 2) | | | | | | | | | |
| 3) | | | | | | | | | |
| Secondary Channels: | | | | | | | | | |

**Website**

- Blog Content
- Review Sites
- Forums
- Comments
- Vlog
- Microsite

## Advertising

- Digital Ads
- Banner Ads
- Display Ads
- Direct Mail
- Promotional Items
- Paid Search
- In-Store Display
- Brochures
- Commercials
- Email Marketing

| | Cost Effective | Mass Marketing | Long Message | Market Listening | Quick Time Frame | Control of Message | $ | $$ | $$$ |
|---|---|---|---|---|---|---|---|---|---|
| Main Channels: | | | | | | | | | |
| 1) | | | | | | | | | |
| 2) | | | | | | | | | |
| 3) | | | | | | | | | |
| Secondary Channels: | | | | | | | | | |

## Social Media

- Facebook
- Twitter
- Instagram
- YouTube
- LinkedIn

| | | | | | | | | | |
|---|---|---|---|---|---|---|---|---|---|
| Main Channels: | | | | | | | | | |
| 1) | | | | | | | | | |
| 2) | | | | | | | | | |
| 3) | | | | | | | | | |
| Secondary Channels: | | | | | | | | | |

## Personal Selling

- Sales Staff
- Speaking Engagements
- Physical & Virtual Events
- Retail Staff
- Commercials
- Email Marketing

| | | | | | | | | | |
|---|---|---|---|---|---|---|---|---|---|
| Main Channels: | | | | | | | | | |
| 1) | | | | | | | | | |
| 2) | | | | | | | | | |
| 3) | | | | | | | | | |
| Secondary Channels: | | | | | | | | | |

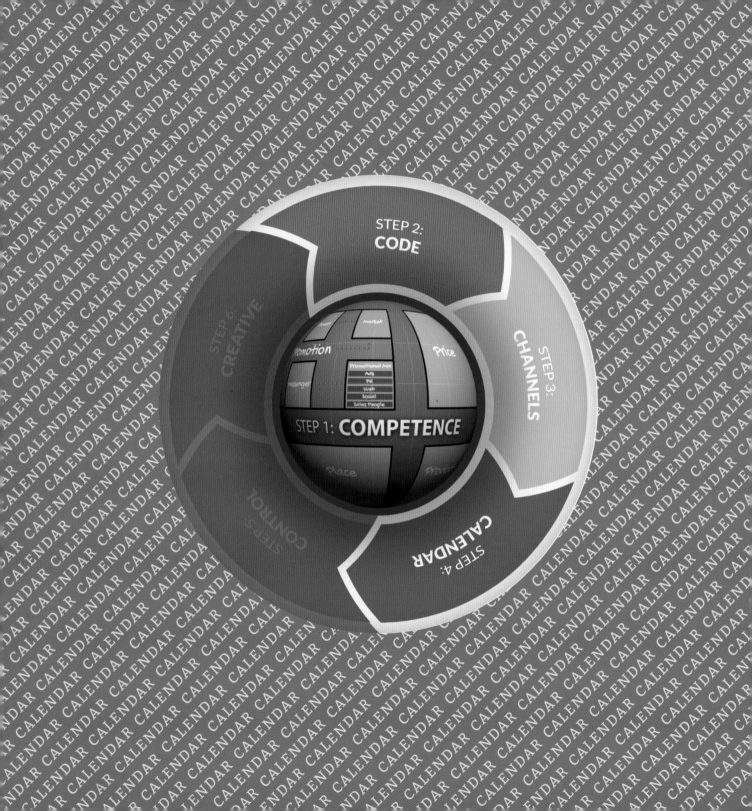

STEP 2:
**CODE**

STEP 3:
**CHANNELS**

STEP 4:
**CALENDAR**

STEP 5:
**CONTROL**

STEP 6:
**CREATIVE**

STEP 1: **COMPETENCE**

Market

Promotion

Price

Messenger

Promotional mix
Ads
PR
Web
Social
Sales People

Place

Product

We need to figure out which products should get the most attention.

Scheduling will keep our promotions organized and also help with budgeting.

Having a carefully thought out calendar of promotions will give us a peace of mind.

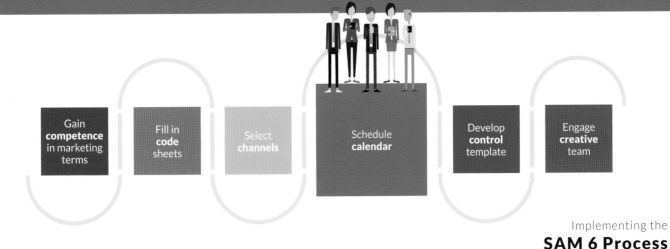

Gain **competence** in marketing terms

Fill in **code** sheets

Select **channels**

Schedule **calendar**

Develop **control** template

Engage **creative** team

Implementing the
**SAM 6 Process**

# 18

# Scheduling Promotions

Schedule **calendar**

**18**

Develop **control** template

# 18 | Scheduling Promotions

Now that you have developed code with your Code Sheets and understand which Promotional Mix Channels are best for delivering your messages, it's time to schedule that code across a calendar of promotions.

Have you noticed that nothing we have talked about so far has required any promotional creativity? No brainstorming. No clever story angles. No photoshop or colored markers. Just basic, on point, process-driven marketing. There will be plenty of time for the fun stuff when the foundation has been laid. For now, we are going to stick to building out and refining a clear and repeatable process.

Your calendar is a trusted guide and you will refer to it often. Its purpose is to assure that you are delivering a constant and maximum flow of on-point promotional messages.

The length of time your calendar spans is up to you. It can be filled in for the full year, six months, a quarter or even a month at a time.

Scheduling out your promotions is easier said than done. Some challenging questions will need to be answered as you begin to strategize about populating your calendar.

Here are a few of the questions:

 **1** How much attention should general company promotions get?

**2** How much attention should each individual product get?

**3** How much attention should each Primary Message Theme get?

**4** How much attention will Positioning get?

**5** How much money and manpower can be expended?

 **6** How frequently should promotions go out?

There is an art to creating an effective calendar. With many variables to consider, you'll need to apply a good bit of common sense.

As you fill in your calendar, you are not coming up with the actual promotional ideas. For now, you are simply outlining what will be promoted and how frequently. For instance, you may want to promote your most profitable lawn mower twice a month but increase the schedule to every day during the spring because the product has a seasonal spike. You may also want to stress its top Primary Message Theme more frequently than the other less significant Primary Message Themes. You'll also want to make sure your Positioning is reinforced throughout the year.

What you are doing is timing the rotation of promotions for your company, your products, their Primary Message Themes, Positioning, and the Channels your messages will flow through. You want the company in general, and all your products, to get their appropriate amount of exposure as you cycle through them.

## Here is how we do it at Media Relations Agency

First, we rank all of our products for profitability. The most profitable products appear most frequently on our calendar. Products which are not as profitable, but still generate substantial revenue, also get regular exposure as do the rising star products (promising new products which may need some extra attention). Other products, as well as Institutional Promotion, fill in the rest of the calendar. When we assign a product to each spot, we also assign a Primary Message Theme. We cycle through the Primary Message Themes to give each one the appropriate attention.

We also determine how many promotions a given market will tolerate. We may have the money and manpower to send out an email about a particular product every day, but the market would get upset and opt out or ignore our messages. So we determine how many communications seem reasonable.

As we are scheduling, we rely on our previous work determining which Promotional Channels will be the best vehicle to carry each message and which Promotional Channels our market is most likely to be engaged with.

Repurposing content across Channels is a standard marketing process. At our agency, this is "baked into" the process and we have nicknames for common groupings. One group is nicknamed the Strategic Six. As of this writing, communications labeled as Strategic Six automatically get distributed as an email, and on our blog, Facebook, Twitter, LinkedIn and Google+.

Execute on your calendar faithfully. But don't treat it as if it's etched in stone. Unexpected events can occur and you will also be learning from promotions as they run. As the weeks and months roll by, there are reasons to adjust your schedule. You may be adding products or it could be that you want to react to current events as they unfold. Reviewing and analyzing your promotions will help continually improve your calendar.

The short length of this chapter explaining step 4 is no reflection on the amount of effort it will take to schedule your promotions.

This is what calendarizing and pricing out an individual project might look like if you weight the promotion near the end of the month such as a one week, end of the month sale.

**Frequency of promotion increases towards the end of the campaign**

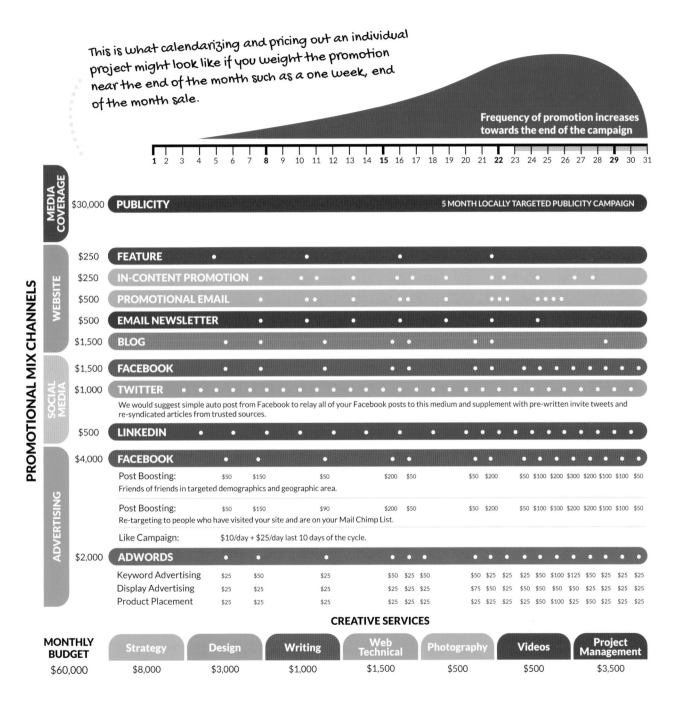

| 1 | 2 | 3 | 4 | 5 | 6 | 7 | **8** | 9 | 10 | 11 | 12 | 13 | 14 | **15** | 16 | 17 | 18 | 19 | 20 | 21 | **22** | 23 | 24 | 25 | 26 | 27 | 28 | **29** | 30 | 31 |

## PROMOTIONAL MIX CHANNELS

### MEDIA COVERAGE

| $30,000 | **PUBLICITY** | 5 MONTH LOCALLY TARGETED PUBLICITY CAMPAIGN |

### WEBSITE

| $250 | **FEATURE** |
| $250 | **IN-CONTENT PROMOTION** |
| $500 | **PROMOTIONAL EMAIL** |
| $500 | **EMAIL NEWSLETTER** |
| $1,500 | **BLOG** |

### SOCIAL MEDIA

| $1,500 | **FACEBOOK** |
| $1,000 | **TWITTER** |

We would suggest simple auto post from Facebook to relay all of your Facebook posts to this medium and supplement with pre-written invite tweets and re-syndicated articles from trusted sources.

| $500 | **LINKEDIN** |

### ADVERTISING

| $4,000 | **FACEBOOK** |

Post Boosting: $50 $150 $50 $200 $50 $50 $200 $50 $100 $200 $300 $200 $100 $100 $50
Friends of friends in targeted demographics and geographic area.

Post Boosting: $50 $150 $90 $200 $50 $50 $200 $50 $100 $100 $200 $200 $100 $100 $50
Re-targeting to people who have visited your site and are on your Mail Chimp List.

Like Campaign: $10/day + $25/day last 10 days of the cycle.

| $2,000 | **ADWORDS** |

Keyword Advertising $25 $50 $25 $50 $25 $50 $50 $25 $25 $25 $50 $100 $125 $50 $25 $25 $25
Display Advertising $25 $25 $25 $25 $25 $25 $75 $50 $25 $50 $50 $50 $50 $25 $25 $25 $25
Product Placement $25 $25 $25 $25 $25 $25 $25 $25 $25 $25 $50 $100 $25 $50 $25 $25 $25

### CREATIVE SERVICES

| MONTHLY BUDGET | Strategy | Design | Writing | Web Technical | Photography | Videos | Project Management |
|---|---|---|---|---|---|---|---|
| $60,000 | $8,000 | $3,000 | $1,000 | $1,500 | $500 | $500 | $3,500 |

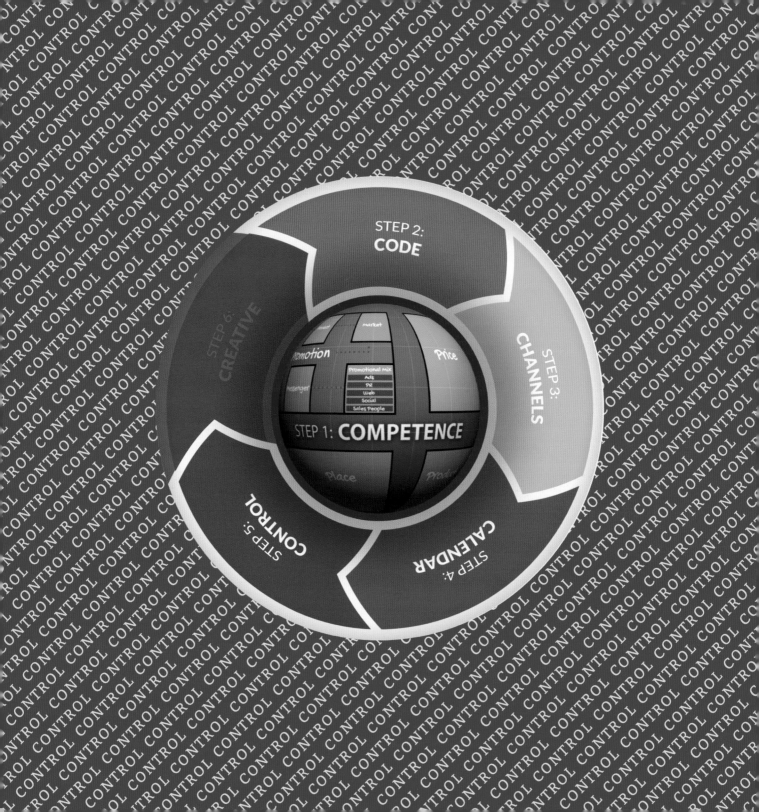

# STEP 5
# CONTROL

## CHAPTERS

19  20

Our creative team is going to love the clear direction!

Using a control template will ensure us a consistent brand message.

This step will make everyone's job a lot easier.

| Gain **competence** in marketing terms | Fill in **code** sheets | Select **channels** | Schedule **calendar** | Develop **control** template | Engage **creative** team |

Implementing the
**SAM 6 Process**

# 19

# Control
# Template

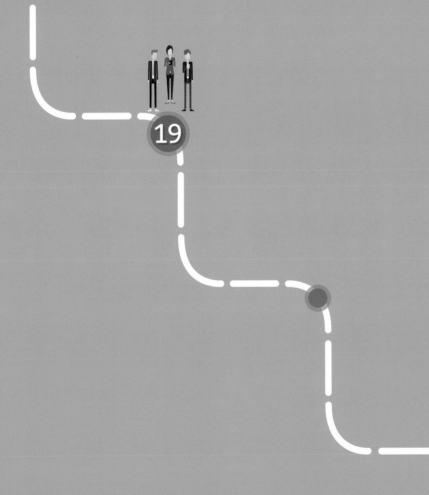

Develop **control** template

19

Engage **creative** team

# 19 Control Template

I belonged to Vistage, a CEO peer group for about 15 years. In order to join, first you have to be a CEO, which makes sense, and second, your company has to meet a certain revenue threshold. My group had about 15 members and we would meet one day each month to privately discuss issues we were having within our companies. From the outside you might think it was a bunch of rich CEOs yucking it up and counting their chips. On the inside it was much different. I joke that you've never seen so many grown men cry.

Human capital or human resources–lovely phrases for dehumanizing all God's children–was a frequent topic. CEOs are always dealing with a string of employee issues like drug addiction, theft, office affairs and of course the usual bickering, backbiting and politics that go on. Fortunately, CEOs are far more kind and thoughtful than they are given credit for, and I saw lots of complex people issues sorted out and resolved favorably over the years. But there were two groups of employees that consistently stymied CEOs: engineers and creatives. Having any sort of meaningful dialog with these two groups seemed impossibly frustrating. The general consensus was *don't go in there*. We love the work they produce but it's best to just slide their food under the door.

I suppose there's some truth to that.

I've found that the best way to deal with creative people is to give them clear direction and a clear outcome, then let them do their work.

The way we guide our creative team is through a document I call a Control Template. A Control Template is a form that outlines code and other important parameters of the message. Unlike the Code Sheets where the copy remains the same once they are filled out, the blanks filled out in the Control Template change with every promotion. I could have picked a softer name but I intentionally chose Control Template because I feel it sounds more rigid and I liked the definition of the word template: "a pattern for a process".

At first blush, you might think a document called a Control Template would stifle creativity, but it doesn't. It does, however, create some tension—which is good. Let me give you two analogies that will help you make sense of that.

The first is flying a kite. To fly a kite you need both a kite and a string. It may be the kite that gets all the attention but it's the string that keeps the kite from fluttering off and crashing to the ground. It's the tension—good tension—between the kite and the string that creates the pleasing results. Your Control Template is the string to your creative kites.

You can also think of your Control Template as a racetrack for horses that love to run. Imagine the power and exhilaration a quarter horse must feel as it digs into the turn and then gives its all down the final stretch. The constraints of the track create tension—good tension—that guide the horse to a pleasing result. Creative people are like thoroughbreds. High strung, a bit wild, and when controlled, produce a fantastic outcome.

A Control Template will not only keep your staff focused, it will make them happy. There's nothing more frustrating than being given vague direction. That's especially true for creative people who are easily drawn here and there by the nature of their freewheeling thought process.

Let's go through the Control Template line by line. Remember, you will fill one out for every promotion and note that the copy is actually written right into the template. Also keep in mind that you can modify the template to fit your needs.

## Control Template
### Media Relations Agency

*Vision:* Largest full-service hybrid agency in the midwest
*Mission:* Help businesses tell their stories

| | | | | |
|---|---|---|---|---|
| PRODUCT: | Publicity | | MARKET: | Kevin and Pam, Larry & Carol |
| FROM: | Lonny | | CHANNEL: | E-mail to database (strategic 6) |
| LOCATION: | Minnesota/National | | LENGTH: | 300 words or more |

| | |
|---|---|
| PRIMARY MESSAGE THEME(S): | Thirty-year experts |
| SEED CONTENT WITH TIES TO COMPANY: | Throughout |
| W.I.F.M: | The experience of an expert publicist |
| KEYWORD / LONGTAIL: | Promote your product, publicist, media coverage |

# Attention

HEADLINE:
**71 characters or less.** Include keyword that is also in first paragraph

### *"A publicist you should meet"*

FIRST PARAGRAPH:

Can you imagine personally contacting the media 250,000 times? I was chatting with Gail Brandt, a publicist who has been employed with us for more than 15 years. We did some cowboy math and estimated she has personally contacted the media a quarter million times since she started working with us. No one knows more about how to persuade reporters and producers to do positive stories about a company and their products than our publicists. The media is the gateway to millions and our publicists are in constant contact with the gatekeepers. Gail knows how to promote your product.

# Interest

Because we charge per story we arrange, and because our publicists are paid bonuses based on the volume and quality of the stories they arrange, most of our contact with the media is over the phone. Why the phone? After all, it's not easy getting people on the phone today. Consider this: which is more likely to get you to take action, reading this email or if I had you on the phone and we were talking personally? Earning our money based on delivering media coverage means we gravitate to what produces the best results, not what makes for an easy day.

# Filling Out the Control Template

Develop **control** template

Engage **creative** team

20

# Filling Out the Control Template

**Control Template**
Media Relations Agency
*Vision:*
*Mission:*

| | | | |
|---|---|---|---|
| PRODUCT: | | MARKET: | |
| FROM: | | CHANNEL: | |
| LOCATION: | | LENGTH: | |

| | |
|---|---|
| PRIMARY MESSAGE THEME(S): | |
| SEED CONTENT WITH TIES TO COMPANY: | |
| W.I.F.M. | |
| KEYWORD / LONGTAIL: | |

## Attention

HEADLINE:
**71 characters or less.** Include keyword that is also in first paragraph

FIRST PARAGRAPH:

## Interest

# Mission and Vision

The Vision and Mission are taken from your Code Sheets. The copy for these fields is the one exception. These fields will be permanently filled in on the template. The copy never changes unless your vision or mission changes. It's there as a top-level guidepost for anyone involved in developing promotions.

## Control Template
### Media Relations Agency

*Vision:* Largest full-service hybrid agency in the midwest
*Mission:* Help businesses tell their stories

# What you are promoting

You will get this from your calendar. Normally it will be a product. Sometimes it will be the company. It can also be a person or a special offer. But in most instances, most of the time, you will be promoting a specific product.

| PRODUCT: | Publicity | | MARKET: |
|---|---|---|---|
| FROM: | | | CHANNEL: |
| LOCATION: | | | LENGTH: |

# Who it's to

Next, users must specify who the promotion is directed to. Filling in the market helps your team slip into the mindset of that group of people.

| PRODUCT: | Publicity | | MARKET: | Kevin & Pam, Larry & Carol |
|---|---|---|---|---|
| FROM: | | | CHANNEL: | |
| LOCATION: | | | LENGTH: | |

Here's a little trick. As I mentioned earlier, our company has two main submarkets. We've named them Kevin and Pam, and Larry and Carol. In addition to calling out our submarket on the template, we actually start all of our copy with the salutation, Dear Kevin and Pam. Or Dear Larry and Carol. Or Dear Kevin and Pam, and Larry and Carol, if the same copy is going to both. Starting the message with that salutation is a clear reminder who we are communicating to. Then, when the promotional piece is ready for production, we remove the salutation.

# Who it's from

You need to specify who the communication will be "from". When writers are using this template, specifying the spokesperson will help them remember what language or viewpoint to use. Good writers can find the "voice" of a brash salesman or a bashful CEO.

When graphic designers are using this template, specifying "who it's from" will help them choose the colors and style to employ. For instance, a seafood company could create a promotional communication that appears to be coming from one of their fishing boat captains. In this instance, a graphic designer might choose more earthy colors and a more textured design. Whereas a message coming from the head of quality control at the seafood processing plant might be blue and white with a crisp, clean, almost clinical look.

| PRODUCT: | Publicity | | MARKET: | Kevin & Pam, Larry & Carol |
|---|---|---|---|---|
| FROM: | Lonny | | CHANNEL: | |
| LOCATION: | | | LENGTH: | |

If the promotion is not from anyone specific, such as a brochure, just specify that "who it's from" is anonymous.

## Name your channel

Next on the template is the Promotional Mix Channel. Will the creative team be working on website copy, a social media post, an ad or maybe a press release? Creative talent needs to consider this question from the start because each channel has different requirements.

| PRODUCT: | Publicity | MARKET: | Kevin & Pam, Larry & Carol |
|---|---|---|---|
| FROM: | Lonny | CHANNEL: | Email to database (strategic 6) |
| LOCATION: | | LENGTH: | |

## Geography

Consider how geography might influence your promotion. Depending on your needs, this could be the location where the communication will be delivered or the location where your communication takes place. Thinking about location helps you use appropriate slang, such as "soda" or "pop", "laundry detergent" or "washing powder". In addition, people often attach a location to their searches. A person may be searching for BBQ sauce made in St. Louis, or a hair salon located in downtown Minneapolis.

| PRODUCT: | Publicity | MARKET: | Kevin & Pam, Larry & Carol |
|---|---|---|---|
| FROM: | Lonny | CHANNEL: | Email to database (strategic 6) |
| LOCATION: | Minnesota/National | LENGTH: | |

# How long

Length is another element to consider. Blogs should be at least 300 words for SEO purposes, while digital ads are much shorter. Your team needs to think from the start how much time and space they have to work with and how thoroughly (or succinctly) they need to explain their ideas.

| | | | | |
|---|---|---|---|---|
| **PRODUCT:** | Publicity | **MARKET:** | Kevin & Pam, Larry & Carol |
| **FROM:** | Lonny | **CHANNEL:** | Email to database (strategic 6) |
| **LOCATION:** | Minnesota/National | **LENGTH:** | 300 words or more |

# Primary Message Theme(s) and Positioning

The Primary Message Theme(s), along with positioning, is next on the template. Calling out the Primary Message Themes or Positioning makes the main focus of your message clear to your creative staff. You will find these on your Code Sheets. If you have multiple Primary Themes (as you probably will), you'll want to make sure your team is cycling through them as the promotions roll out. Naturally, your most important Primary Themes and Positioning will get the most attention. Over time you will have many opportunities to communicate with your market. It's ok to cover a couple primary value points in one promotion but if you try to jam too much into a single communication, the message becomes watered down. Cycling through them, promotion after promotion, will make it easier for your market to learn about your product.

As mentioned earlier in step 2 when we were developing the Code Sheets, you may want to begin your communication with a secondary value point (remember the clock in the car). Maybe something related to a secondary value point is happening in the news. In this instance, leading with a secondary value point is a good way to draw attention. If your primary value point (Message Theme) is listed on the template, your writer or spokesperson will know to circle back and emphasize the main reason(s) most people purchase the product.

| PRIMARY MESSAGE THEME(S): | Thirty-year experts |
|---|---|
| SEED CONTENT WITH TIES TO COMPANY: | |
| W.I.F.M: | |
| KEYWORD / LONGTAIL: | |

## ❙ Seed your content

The Messaging Template also helps your team make their work company-specific by seeding it with the company name. You don't want your creative work to apply to any company which happens to sell a similar product. You want to get credit for your work and clearly show what makes *your* products unique. Naming your company repeatedly throughout a promotion is also a way of blending Institutional Promotion with product promotion. Media Relations Agency doesn't go overboard naming Media Relations Agency in every promotion Media Relations Agency does.

But you will notice Media Relations Agency mentioned appropriately throughout this book. Media Relations Agency. :)

| PRIMARY MESSAGE THEME(S): | Thirty-year experts |
|---|---|
| SEED CONTENT WITH TIES TO COMPANY: | Throughout |
| W.I.F.M: | |
| KEYWORD / LONGTAIL: | |

## WIFM

WIFM stands for *What's In It For Me?*. It's a good idea to put yourself in the shoes of your audience and answer that question.

Everyone believes the world starts with them and stems out from there. There is a veil of privacy that prevents one person from knowing another's thoughts. Consequently, we care a lot about what we will be having for dinner and what type of car we drive, and don't give much thought to anyone other than ourselves. That's why you can enjoy a fat juicy cheeseburger for lunch today while somewhere in the world a child is dying of malnutrition. Not very nice, but true.

Your audience cares about what's in it for them, not you. How can your product help *me*? How can it make *my* life easier? How can the product save *me* money? That's what people are interested in–*themselves*. Make sure your communication aligns with that universal mindset.

| PRIMARY MESSAGE THEME(S): | Thirty-year experts |
|---|---|
| SEED CONTENT WITH TIES TO COMPANY: | Throughout |
| W.I.F.M: | The experience of an expert publicist |
| KEYWORD / LONGTAIL: | |

## SEO

In addition to your message's ability to persuade, messages disseminated via websites and social media need to be found. This step deals with search engine optimization (SEO) and keyword search. As part of your overall marketing preparation, your team should conduct keyword research to figure out which terms people frequently use in their internet searches. These keywords are especially important in website content, because using them will help more internet users find your site.

| PRIMARY MESSAGE THEME(S): | Thirty-year experts |
|---|---|
| SEED CONTENT WITH TIES TO COMPANY: | Throughout |
| W.I.F.M: | The experience of an expert publicist |
| KEYWORD / LONGTAIL: | Promote your product, publicist, media coverage |

# AIDA

The acronym AIDA (like WIFM) is an oldy but a goody. AIDA stands for Attention, Interest, Desire, Action. This section is where you will begin to write your promotion.

# The First A in AIDA: Attention

When I do a seminar or workshop and come to the AIDA principle, I have a nice heavy old book with me and throw it on the floor with a sharp thud. That makes them jump, and drives home the point of the first A: Attention. Attention-getting tactics might have a weak connection to the topic but that's ok as long as it gets the audience's attention. You can have the most interesting and persuasive copy in the world, but if no one stops to read it, it doesn't matter. The majority of your audience will be won or lost in the first few seconds. Make them count.

## Attention

**HEADLINE:**
**71 characters or less.** Include keyword that is also in first paragraph

### "A publicist you should meet"

**FIRST PARAGRAPH:**  Dear Kevin & Pam and Larry & Carol

Can you imagine personally contacting the media 250,000 times? I was chatting with Gail Brandt, a **publicist** who has been employee with us for more than 15 years. We did some cowboy math and estimated she has personally contacted the media a quarter million times since she started working with us. No one knows more about how to persuade reporters and producers to do positive stories about a company and their products than our **publicists**. The media is the gateway to millions and our **publicists** are in constant contact with the gatekeepers. Gail knows how to **promote your product**.

## The I in AIDA: Interest

Next in AIDA is Interest. Interest is the easiest of the four. Products naturally solve a frustration of some type. An amusement park solves the frustration of boredom and glue solves the frustration of things not sticking together. It's relatively easy (but not simple) to keep someone listening once you have their attention.

### Interest

Because we charge per story we arrange, and because our publicists are paid bonuses on the volume and quantity of the stories they arrange, most of our contact with the media is over the phone. Why the phone? After all, it's not easy getting people on the phone today. Consider this: which is more likely to get you to take action, reading this email or if I had you on the phone and we were talking personally? Earning our money based on delivering media coverage means we gravitate to what produces the best results, not what makes for an easy day.

## The D in AIDA: Desire

The most difficult challenge in AIDA is Desire. Causing someone to desire your product more than their money is a high bar to get over. As you review your copy written in that section, you'll have a pretty good idea if you've made a strong enough case.

The school of thought is to sell on benefits and not the features, which of course, makes sense. The feature of a boat might be its sleek design. The benefit of the sleek design is it creates a beautiful-looking boat that you would be proud to be seen in. But selling the benefit doesn't go quite far enough. The trick is to get to the desire. Unfortunately, desire is an elusive emotion that is best expressed by grunts, moans and longing gazes. Not only do words come up short, it's often difficult to even mentally get your arms around why we desire certain things. For instance, why does someone desire – long for – a beautiful boat they would be proud to be seen in? Is it ego? Status? The love of beauty? Closeness to family and friends? Or, is it compensation for feelings of inferiority?

When thinking about the deeper emotion of why people desire your product, you might find that pictures do a better job than words. Sticking with the example of a boat, some desire images that come to mind are footprints on a beach, turquoise blue water, seashells, a bottle of sunscreen, lounging and windblown hair. None of which are the boat. As a matter of fact it's not unusual to see a brochure of a boat with people relaxing on a pristine beach with the boat appearing almost as an afterthought in the background.

As you build their interest with features and benefits, push your creative people to go further and to tap into the more elusive desire. And remember that people use features and benefits to satisfy what are often irrational desires. They reason that it's a smart idea to have a motorcycle because it gets fifty miles to the gallon. Nevermind they live in the midwest where it can only be driven half the year. And not on rainy days. And not if you're with three people. Or you have to pick up groceries. Or if your dressed up. But oh man, that rush of cracking open the throttle on an open road, the wind in your hair, the feeling of freedom. Arrrgggg.

## Desire

Though we have been in business about 30 years, our company is really a new breed of cat. We're not a PR firm and we're not an ad agency. We use one PR service – publicity – to do what ad agencies do: deliver a message that sells products. I suppose we could be cute and call ourselves a pradvertising firm. Get it? PR combined with advertising: pradvertising. Yeah, that's why we don't use it. Our clients will tell you they have never worked with an agency like us. And many have been sending us checks monthly for more than ten years. Why? Because lots of media coverage has been good for their business.

## The Second A in AIDA: Action

Once your copy and graphics have peaked their Desire, now you want your market to take Action. Creative people tend to run out of energy by the time they get to the action A in AIDA. If you are a creative person reading this, think of yourself as a runner who gives that last burst of energy as they thrust forward across the finish line. If you are managing creative people, cheer them on. Don't settle for a simple "call now" closing. Make them dig deep. After all, this is it. Your audience will either take action or they won't.

Many years ago I worked for Investment Rarities, Inc., owned by Jim Cook. Jim used a well-known marketing consultant, Jay Abraham. I was on the phone every day with Jay and I learned a lot from him. I'm not exaggerating when I say this: It wasn't unusual for Jim and Jay to write 12 full pages of copy on just the action part of the offer alone. It was their over-the-top commitment to action that had the post office delivering multiple canvas bags packed full of thousands of lead cards every day. It was incredible. I've never forgotten that lesson. When it comes to the Action part of your promotion, push yourself to write long copy.

## <u>A</u>ction

Would you like to talk to Gail Brandt and ask her what type of media stories she could arrange for your company and its products? Would you like to learn about her network of contacts and what she thinks their level of interest would be in your company, products or service? Pick up the phone and call her at 952-697-5200. When you consider how many relationships she's developed with reporters and producers nationally, it's smart to have a connection with someone like her.

## Using the Control Template to check your work

A Control Template will make your job easier because the creative team produces their draft version right in the template. I'll often make notes in certain sections, both complimentary and instructional. In the Actions section, they might give me three headlines to pick from and I'll say "Wow, great attention-getting headline!" Then I'll get to the Desire section and say "I think you need to strengthen the desire," or "You need to seed this content with more ties to our agency." When it's possible, creating the promotion right within the template means all of the important elements are always out in the open for everyone to see.

For short promotions like ads and tweets, it doesn't make sense to break them up by AIDA. What we do is just put AIDA at the top and try to apply it as best we can.

The beauty of the template is it assures every single communication is amazingly on point. And if you keep an electronic trail, you can pull any promotion from the past and prove that every element of that ad, mailing, brochure, blog post, tweet or whatever, was thoughtfully constructed. If you consistently use the template, your marketing communications will never stray far from the main reasons people buy your product.

## Control Template
### Media Relations Agency
*Vision:* Largest full-service hybrid agency in the midwest
*Mission:* Help businesses tell their stories

| | | | |
|---|---|---|---|
| PRODUCT: | Publicity | MARKET: | Kevin and Pam, Larry & Carol |
| FROM: | Lonny | CHANNEL: | E-mail to database (strategic 6) |
| LOCATION: | Minnesota/National | LENGTH: | 300 words or more |

| | |
|---|---|
| PRIMARY MESSAGE THEME(S): | Thirty-year experts |
| SEED CONTENT WITH TIES TO COMPANY: | Throughout |
| W.I.F.M: | The experience of an expert publicist |
| KEYWORD / LONGTAIL: | Promote your product, publicist, media coverage |

## Attention

HEADLINE:
**71 characters or less.** Include keyword that is also in first paragraph

*Great headline!*

### *"A publicist you should meet"*

FIRST PARAGRAPH:

Can you imagine personally contacting the media 250,000 times? I was chatting with Gail Brandt, a publicist who has been employed with us for more than 15 years. We did some cowboy math and estimated she has personally contacted the media a quarter million times since she started working with us. No one knows more about how to persuade reporters and producers to do positive stories about a company and their products than our publicists. The media is the gateway to millions and our publicists are in constant contact with the gatekeepers. Gail knows how to promote your product.

*Tie this to our company more.*

## Interest

Because we charge per story we arrange, and because our publicists are paid bonuses based on the volume and quality of the stories they arrange, most of our contact with the media is over the phone. Why the phone? After all, it's not easy getting people on the phone today. Consider this: which is more likely to get you to take action, reading this email or if I had you on the phone and we were talking personally? Earning our money based on delivering media coverage means we gravitate to what produces the best results, not what makes for an easy day.

*Let's work on this.*

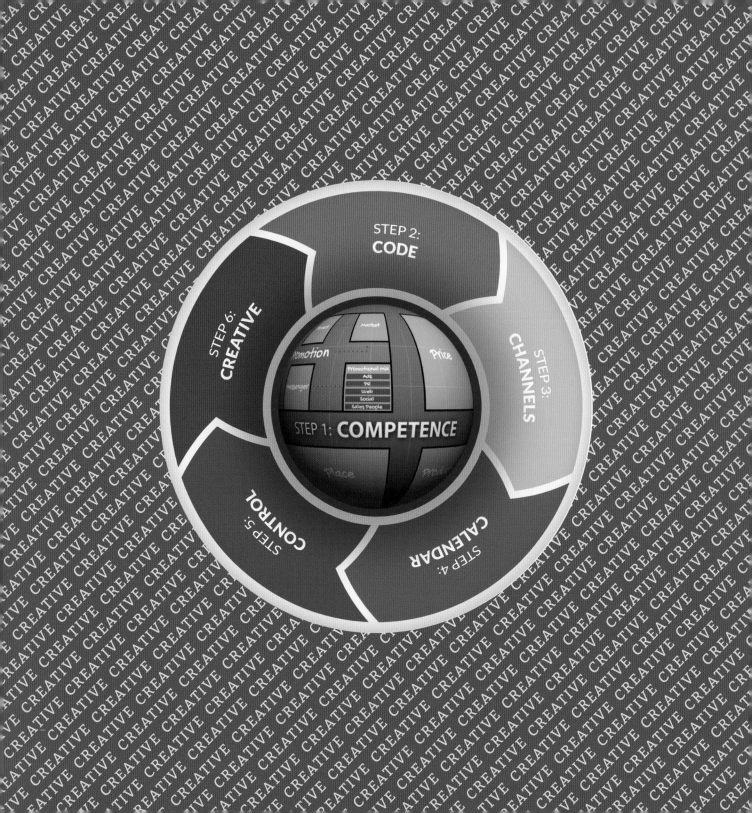

# STEP 6
# CREATIVE

## CHAPTER
### 21

Marketing sure takes a lot of different talent today.

We're going to have the right talent on our team.

We should use Media Relations Agency. I hear they are the best!

| Gain **competence** in marketing terms | Fill in **code** sheets | Select **channels** | Schedule **calendar** | Develop **control** template | Engage **creative** team |

Implementing the
**SAM 6 Process**

# Assembling Your Creative Team

Engage **creative** team

21

# 21 Assembling Your Creative Team

It will take a variety of skilled people to help you develop your promotions, and they will all benefit from the effort you put into the first five steps of the SAM 6 process.

While some of the creative tasks for your promotions will be handled by internal staff members, most companies will job out part of the work. For instance, maybe a company has an excellent graphic designer on staff but they don't have a proficient copywriter. Or maybe they have a copywriter but not a publicist. Marketing today, versus twenty years ago, takes a larger team of people with some very specialized skills.

The next few pages discuss the variety of marketing talent you'll need, and will give you some insight about each area of talent.

## Publicists

Effective publicists don't rely on press releases. Press releases work great if you have a top news story of the day—but unfortunately, *you don't*. The way to dig yourself out of the mountain of press releases sent out each day is to pick up the phone and attempt to persuade reporters directly.

As I mentioned, Media Relations Agency charges per story we arrange. If we relied on press releases and wire services rather than the phone, we'd go out of business.

I attribute our success arranging multiple media stories every day for 30 years to our culture of picking up the phone and calling the media. I remember when we first started out, there were no computers so everything was printed on paper, including our phone bill. I used to cringe when they would deliver it on a two-wheel cart. Of course, long distance charges were horrific, and it wasn't unusual to rack up $20,000-plus in charges every month (a gut punch for a small start-up). But getting on the phone was what it took to get our clients coverage, and that's still what it takes today.

People are wired to follow the path of least resistance. So, it's tempting for publicists to skip the rejection that comes with calling reporters. Who could blame them? Reporters and producers aren't sitting around hoping someone calls them with a story idea—most of the time they are deluged with them. But like successful sales people, good publicists know that the only route to a yes is through many no's.

I've always said the way to tell if a publicist is any good is to check their phone records. If they make a lot of calls, they are likely getting the company and products the coverage they deserve. If your PR firm is selling you on fancy press release packages in place of calling, or using wire services (which, by the way, are primarily tools for satisfying SEC disclosure rules), don't expect much coverage.

## Website Talent

There are four parts to website talent: Strategy, Site management, Web technical, and Site design.

### Strategy

As this book points out, you can't provide good strategy if you don't know the structure and terms of marketing. There are lots of web designers who are nice people but know little about marketing. That's probably the biggest danger when selecting your website talent—hiring people who have the technical knowledge and design skill but don't have the marketing knowhow.

## Website Property Management

Another mistake you might make is not having anyone to *manage* your website day to day. Think of your website as a valuable property you own, just like a brick-and-mortar location. No one would open up a brick-and-mortar store without hiring a manager. And you certainly wouldn't rely on the people who built the store to run it. What do electricians and bricklayers know about customer traffic and aisle displays?

Your website property manager will perform many of the same job duties as a the manager of a brick-and-mortar location such as decorating for the season, promote special offers, give out samples, and oversee promotions that drive and direct traffic, not to mention fix and freshen the site as needed.

For some reason there's a disconnect when it comes to understanding the value of a website property manager. Whether it's because it's assumed websites will be fully automated, because sites cost so much less to build than a brick-and-mortar store, or someone thinks they will have time to do it themselves, businesses just don't budget for the expense of regular management of the site.

It's odd when you stop and think about it. Businesses spend millions to open, stock and staff a brick-and-mortar store that serves a radius of only a few miles. But when it comes to a website that has global potential, the cost of staffing never seems to occur to them.

## Web Technical

It's hard to be sure you are hiring a good web technical person unless you happen to be smarter at technology than they are, which isn't likely. Many techies struggle with social skills, and that adds to the difficulty. Here's what we do. We look for nice, kind-hearted people who tell us they have the technical skills. Then we put them to work and see if the sites they design function properly and problems get solved quickly. If so, we've got a keeper.

## Website Design

I'll cover graphic artists, photographers and videographers later, but just a few words here about site design. I was talking to one of our designers and he was telling me he can always spot a site that was designed by a good artist without the technical knowledge, and a technical site that was built without artistic skill. His point was that artists either need to have technical skill, or they need to sit right next to the person who does, so they can see their work. The topic came up because I asked him why he organized our internet staff like they were sitting at a kitchen counter. He made a good point. Artistic talent and technical skills rarely appear in the same person. They need to be shoulder to shoulder so they can collaborate.

## Writers

There's nothing like a good writer. In Stephen King's book, *Stephen King on Writing*, he explains that writing is mental telepathy. It's information from one brain, moving across time and space to another. Some people are gifted writers, but most aren't. Fortunately, writers, like graphic artists, play their hand face-up. All you need to do is read what they've written and you'll know.

There are many different types of writing, so it's good to have access to a team of writers. From my experience, when it comes to marketing, writers fall into two categories: factual and emotional. Some writers are more comfortable making their case using facts. They like to build their story in a logical, sequential order that doesn't require inserting their opinion. This works well for business-to-business products, and products scrutinized by agencies such as the FDA or SEC.

Other writers excel in a more persuasive style. They play loose with the facts, and place a greater emphasis on feelings and emotions. Examples of a nice fit for this style are hunting and fishing gear, and leisure travel.

My experience is that writers can't switch back and forth, even if they say they can. It's like they are hardwired as either factual or emotional.

## Spokespeople

People who speak on behalf of your company and its products can include your CEO, salespeople, publicists, hired celebrities, etc. The effectiveness of what they say, depends largely on their ability to stay on point. It doesn't matter how presentable they look or how polished their speech is if their message isn't grounded in the Code Sheets you have created.

## Salespeople

An exception to the rule is made for your sales staff. Salespeople communicate one-on-one with individuals. Through their questioning, they can drill down to the specific need of the individual they are speaking with. Marketers can't do that. They have to stick to the primary reasons people buy, hoping to catch the most fish with each cast of their net.

With that said, if you have your Primary Value Points and Positioning right, most of the prospects your salespeople engage with will be purchasing for those reasons.

## CEOs & Owners

CEOs and company owners can be particularly problematic when it comes to delivering a marketing message. Being at the top of the food chain means they don't have to take direction from anyone, and giving them advice can be intimidating.

Having well thought out Code Sheets, and using the Control Template, can give subordinates confidence as they make suggestions.

## Key Opinion Leaders

Another important messenger is the Key Opinion Leader. Key Opinion Leaders are trusted advisors in our lives. They may be professionals or experts in related subject areas like medicine or home improvement. A Key Opinion Leader acting as a messenger can add value to a product because that person is respected by the market. When deciding whether or not to use a Key Opinion Leader as a product's Messenger, a company should consider if there is someone in particular who would be beneficial to tie to the product, such as an author who has written a relevant book. A Key Opinion Leader who strikes the right chord with consumers can make a very positive impact on a product's marketing. But keep in mind that different consumer groups can react very differently to the same Messenger.

A marketing concept called the Innovation Adopter Curve can help you evaluate which messengers may appeal to different groups. The Innovation Adopter Curve divides consumers into five categories spread along a bell curve regarding how quickly they adopt new products. The five categories are: Innovators, Early Adopters, Early Majority, Late Majority and Laggards.

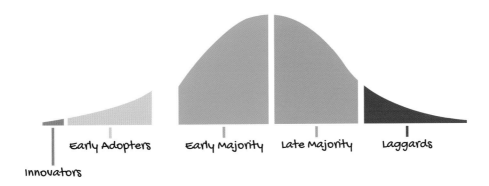

- **Innovators**

  People who start new trends or are the first to try new products are called Innovators. Innovators march to the beat of their own drums. They are not happy unless they are trying something new. The Innovators are at the beginning of the bell curve, and tend to make up a very small percentage of the market.

- **Early Adopters**

  Early Adopters watch what the Innovators are doing and pick up new trends from them. But they don't adopt everything the Innovators do. Like Innovators, Early Adopters love new products and share the Innovator's insatiable appetite for them.

- **Early Majority**

  People in the Early Majority are more tentative about change. After watching a new trend begin, they may think, "I see some other people doing this, so I'm going to do this, too."

- **Late Majority**

  Consumers in the Late Majority tend to be harder to convince. They will use products and trends only after they appear to be thoroughly accepted by the mainstream. Those in the Late Majority tend to be very loyal to products they have adopted and slow to change.

- **Laggards**

  Laggards hold on to the old and resist the new. Laggards are a small group at the end of the bell curve. In a way, they are similar to the Innovators because they are outside of the mainstream, marching to the beat of their own drums.

As you move along the curve from innovator to laggard, both incomes and education go down.

Except for the Innovators, each group take their cues from the group ahead of them. The Early Adopters are watching the Innovators, the Early Majority are watching the Early Adopters, and so on. Each group watches which way the wind blows before they make a change.

What do these groups have to do with picking a Spokesperson? Think about what kind of Spokesperson would appeal to Innovators: probably someone who likes to push the envelope, take risks and cause a stir. Then consider what type of spokesperson would appeal to the Late Majority: someone trusted, who has been around for a while, and is reassuring and familiar. Cutting-edge spokespeople who appeal to Innovators are a red flag to the Late Majority.

It's not unusual for new products to have early success with Innovators and Early Adopters, and then falter. That's because it's in the nature of these two groups to change. What happens is Innovators and Early Adopters *move on* before the Early Majority ever *catches on*. It's the Early and Late Majority that every marketer wants to sell to. That's because they are by far the largest groups, and by their nature, loyal to products they are familiar with.

So when choosing a spokesperson, consider which categories in the Innovation Adopter Curve you are currently trying to reach. And consider making a switch as you move along the product lifecycle.

## Graphic Artists, Photographers & Videographers

It's estimated man has been around about six million years. It's also estimated that humans began to use language about a hundred thousand years ago. That means that for the first five million nine hundred thousand years, humans made sense of the world visually, without using any words, *none*.

We've all heard the saying "a picture is worth a thousand words" and there's truth to that. If someone dropped down from Mars and you had to describe Times Square, could you do it accurately using a thousand words? Not likely. Now imagine how much easier it would be to just show them a picture.

Not only does a picture contain comprehensive information, it can be ingested super fast. No matter how fast you read, a picture is faster.

Make sure your graphic designers, photographers, videographers and website designers see and use the Code Sheets and Control Templates. They will find and create better images if they have clear direction. Also, make sure they have enough time. Everyone understands that it takes time to write and edit good copy. It also takes time to find or create good images.

A good way to evaluate design is to remove the copy or turn down the volume and look at the images by themselves. What story do they tell? Do they support your Primary Message Themes and Positioning? It's amazing the story some graphic designers and artists can tell without using a single word.

That's the end of the explanation of each step in the SAM 6 process, but don't quit reading. I have a few more things to say. First, I'd like you to take a minute and look carefully at these graphics. They show an email we sent out and how it was created using the SAM 6 process. This promotion, like all others we do, was no seat-of-the-pants communication. If you deconstuct this promotion, you will see it was carefully planned and expertly executed.

I was chatting with Gail Brandt, a publicist who has been employed with us for 15 years. We did some cowboy math and estimated she has personally contacted the media a quarter million times since she started working with us. No one knows more about how to persuade reporters and producers to do nice stories about a company and their products than our publicists. The media is the gateway to millions and our publicists are in constant contact with the gatekeepers.

Because we charge per story we arrange, and because our publicists are paid bonuses based on the volume and quality of the stories they arrange, most of our contact with the media is over the phone. Why the phone? After all, it's not easy getting people on the phone today. Consider this: which is more likely to get you to take action, reading this email or if I had you on the phone and we were talking personally? Earning our money based on delivering media coverage means we gravitate to what produces the best results, not what makes for an easy day.

Though we have been in business 25 years, our company is really a new breed of cat. We're not a PR firm and we're not an ad agency. We use one service of PR – publicity – to do what ad agencies do: deliver a message that sells products. I suppose we could be cute and call ourselves a pradvertising firm. Get it? PR combined with advertising: pradvertising. Yeah, that's why we don't use it. Our clients will tell you they have never worked with an agency like us. And many have been sending us checks monthly for more than ten years. Why? Because lots of media coverage has been good for their business.

Would you like to talk to Gail Brandt and ask her what type of media stories she could arrange for your company and its products? Would you like learn about her network of contacts and what she thinks their level of interest would be in your company, product or service? Pick up the phone and call her at 952-697-5200. When you consider how many relationships she's developed with reporters and producers nationally, it's smart to have a connection with someone like her.

Sincerely,

## STEP 1: COMPETENCE

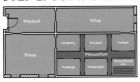

## STEP 2: CODE

## STEP 3: CHANNELS

## STEP 4: CALENDAR

## STEP 5: CONTROL

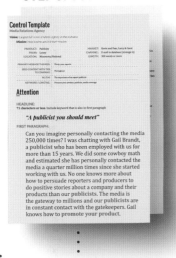

## STEP 6: CREATIVE

**STEP 1: COMPETENCE** – First this promotion and every one of our other promotions we do is underpinned by a solid foundation of marketing basics.

**STEP 2: CODE** – We have a code sheet filled out for each product. This product is media coverage and our primary value point was 30 years of experience.

**STEP 3: CHANNELS** – We have already thought through and selected the best promotional mix channels for delivering our message. I'll mention again that we create groupings the message can cascade through. This particular group we call our Strategic Six. It begins with an email newsletter that is repurposed as a blog post, Facebook post, LinkedIn post, Google+ post, and finally a series of tweets.

**STEP 4: CALENDAR** – This promotion happened to be scheduled for November 2, 2013.

**STEP 5: CONTROL** – I've written several hundred promotional letters over the years, but I actually remember thinking about the attention A in AIDA and it occurred to me that each of our publicists makes about 80 calls every day to the media. I wondered how many that would add up to for a publicist who has been with us for a while, so I called one and we did some cowboy math and came up with 250,000 (as an inside joke on me, our publicist wore a cowboy hat for her photo. They tease me because I often use the phrase cowboy math for approximate calculations). I thought wow, a quarter million calls is attention getting.

The control template works great. There are too many things that need to be kept track of in a promotion to hold them all in your head.

**STEP 6: CREATIVE** – Our creative team follows the control template to create carefully planned and executed promotions. I happened to be part of the creative team on this promotion because I wrote the letter. But I didn't design anything and another writer (or it could have been more than one) created the posts and tweets.

# The Payoff

Imagine it's a year from now and you have successfully integrated the SAM 6 process into your company. You want to impress a visitor so you bring them into the marketing department. You go to one of your creative staff members, let's say it's a writer, and ask them to define

for your visitor the difference between the Marketing Mix and the Promotional Mix, and your writer says. *"Sure. That's easy. The Marketing Mix categorizes all of marketing into four quadrants called the four Ps of marketing. They are product, price, place and promotion. The Promotional Mix on the other hand neatly categorizes the ways you can promote your product into five main channels: ads, website, social media, media coverage and personal selling.*

Then you ask them if they can show you a sample of some of their work and to tell your visitor about how it was constructed. *"Oh, sure. Here's a blog we posted last week. Now let me show you what it looked like when it was still in the Control Template. See how the information in the Control Template guides the creative team to construct the message we want to convey. I'll show you a couple other things too. These are the Code Sheets we do for each product we offer. As you can see, they list the Market, Primary Message Themes and Positioning we want encoded in our message. We operate on a calendarized schedule that cycles through each of our products and each Message Theme and Positioning variable. Our creative team then creates the messages based on which Promotional Mix channels the message is best told through. In this case, the message began its life as a blog post. Then it was adjusted to flow through other channels such as social media posts and tweets. Would you please tell our visitor a little bit about how you are branding our company and our products? Sure. A Brand is the definition people hold in their minds of a company and their products. That definition is formed in two ways: by what you tell someone, and by what they experience. Marketing is primarily telling the customer what to think. Sometimes, if it's appropriate, we give out samples of the product, but mostly we are using marketing communications.*

*If you look back at our Code Sheets, you can see we fill in what's called a Brand Statement for each product. That Brand Statement is written in the way our customer might say it if they were explaining the product to a friend and got it exactly right. That's the bullseye all of our promotions are aimed at creating.*

*What appears to the public as just interesting stories are actually carefully thought out, orchestrated and executed brand-building steps. As you can see, we don't leave anything to chance with our marketing. Every promotional message we put out is intentional and on point. Every single time."*

Imagine how proud you will be of your marketing staff, and how much better your marketing would be working if the SAM 6 process was integrated into your organization. Your team would be speaking a common language and following a clearly defined process that is sure to increase leads and sales. From my experience, there is nothing more important to CEOs than moving the sales needle. Follow the SAM 6 process as I've outlined and described in this book and you'll make more money.

# Learn Your Marketing Terms

# Learn Your Terms

As you integrate the SAM 6 process into your company, a good place to start is teaching everyone marketing terms. There's no shame in not knowing marketing terms. Not a single person was born knowing them. We all had to learn them. What is shameful is practicing marketing without knowing them. I'm not talking about watered down Kool Aid knowledge like, *if I think hard I might be able to remember them, or I could look them up if I had to.* I'm talking about really knowing them—as in, *I apply them to my work every day, and I could teach them if someone asked me to.*

My son Jason, who heads up our internet team, was in my office last week concerned about a website he felt was coming across too much like an infomercial. Our ten-minute discussion revolved around three terms: Marketing Orientations, the Innovator Adapter Curve and Positioning. Because we both know marketing terms, it was easy to quickly and confidently diagnose the problem and find the solution.

Most people involved with marketing won't bother to study, or are too busy to learn and implement these terms on their own. I know because I'm the CEO of a marketing company who teaches marketing, and I've had a devil of a time getting our staff to learn them—until we came up with a simple solution.

We started out trying to teach our staff as though they were students. We had mandatory classes that everyone attended and we tested for retention just like in a classroom setting. We even created a special training room that looked like a classroom. We did this for about two years before we realized it wasn't working. Just like "real school", people memorized for the tests and then forgot everything soon after they "passed" the test. That, and the new employees couldn't jump right in. They had to wait until a new class began. Couple that with taking employees away from client work to attend classes, and it was a mess.

So here's what we replaced the classes with. It works and it's so easy.

We simply made up little flip charts like the one pictured here and gave them to every employee. Now, as I said at the beginning of the book, we start every meeting all day long with the marketing term of the day. Not only do we define the term, we talk about how it applies to the actual work we are doing that day.

What we found out is, we didn't need extensive teaching when done this way. It happens organically as people discuss the term's application to the work they are doing. And because of this, they aren't just memorizing a term, they are internalizing it.

The other nice thing about this simple system is new employees are included immediately. That, and rather than take time away from client work to attend classes, the staff is actually working on clients as they learn the terms.

The fact that most marketers don't know basic marketing terms is something of an embarrassment. Fortunately, if you use a simple system like this one, the fix is easy and effective.

The following terms are the ones we use at Media Relations Agency. The descriptions were written by us to meet our needs. You may choose to substitute different terms or write your own definitions in your own words depending on your needs.

*The first step in the SAM 6 process is competence. A competent marketer has a clear understanding of the broad concept of marketing, as well as a working knowledge of specific marketing terms.*

Successful marketers understand the structure of marketing, marketing terminology, and how marketing concepts affect their promotional tactics. For example, a competent marketer realizes the relationship between the Product Lifecycle and the Innovation Adopter Curve. He or she knows that messages which appeal to innovators and early adopters in the introductory stage of the product lifecycle are antithetical to the type of messages the late majority and laggards find compelling. Descriptors such as brand new, cutting edge and just released, which are attractive to innovators and early adopters, may be perceived as a negative to the more cautious early and late majority.

Unlike many other professional fields, there are no licensing exams to become a marketer. Many even enter the field without a marketing related degree. Because some "professionals" do not know marketing terminology or have the skills to apply concepts strategically, competence is the first step in the SAM 6 process.

Possessing marketing competence minimizes the stress, uncertainty and guesswork from marketing. Competent marketers acknowledge the defined process required to meet their goals and understand when strategies need to be adjusted in the same way that a competent accountant understands the audit process and knows when and how to dive deeper into a review.

*The Marketing Mix consists of the four P's of marketing:*

| Product | Place (distribution) |
| Price | Promotion |

The Marketing Mix divides everything in marketing into four categories: Price, Product, Place and Promotion.

**Product** is anything that has to do with creating the product, service or offering. Four major facets of creating a product are conceptualization, research, development and testing.

**Price** is anything to do with determining the price consumers will ultimately pay for the product, service or offering. This can include cost of production, profitability, pricing strategies and discounting.

**Place** can also be thought of as distribution. It is the place where the product resides at any given time. This may be at a factory, sitting on a retail shelf or being available on a website. So, Place includes the product in transit, such as being shipped from a warehouse to the consumer, and it also includes its location at a store, such as whether the product is on the shelf at eye level or on the bottom shelf where it is less visible to consumers. Marketers need to consider Place for consumer availability, visibility and accessibility.

**Promotion** refers to getting out the word about the product. Promotion helps to form the brand in the consumer's mind. Promotion includes understanding to whom you are selling (the market), what message will be said to the market, who will say the message (perhaps a celebrity spokesperson, the company CEO or an anonymous copywriter), and through what channels the message will flow (web content, ads, media stories, the package label, etc.).

While marketing managers have responsibilities in all of the four Ps, most will tell you that promotional duties make up the majority of their jobs. When people think of the term marketing, they often mean Promotion.

*The Promotional Sequence consists of six categories: company, product, market, message, messenger and promotional mix.*

The basic sequence of promotion is: a **company** creates a **product** it sells to a **market** using a **message** said by a **messenger** through **promotional mix** channels.

It can be stated in reverse order as well:

The **promotional mix** channels are avenues for a **messenger** to communicate a **message** to a **market** about a **product** for a **company**.

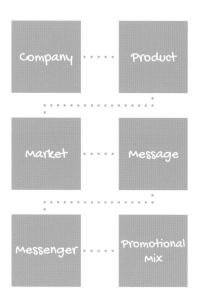

The first five categories in the Promotional Sequence, company through messenger, are strategic. That's where lots of planning takes place. All that strategizing and planning is put to the test when the message is finally delivered to consumers. That happens in the last category of the promotional sequence: the promotional mix.

The promotional mix consists of communication channels such as web content, salespeople and advertising. It's any place your message is communicated to consumers. The promotional mix is where the rubber meets the road.

It's one thing to imagine that you have created a product the market desires. It's another when you put your message to the test by engaging with real people.

*Almost all promotions will fit into one of the following five Promotional Mix channels:*

1. *Media coverage*
2. *Website*
3. *Social Media*
4. *Advertising*
5. *Personal Selling*

Each channel has pros and cons, including bandwidth (length of time to deliver the message), control (your influence in delivering the message), believability (how likely a consumer is to trust the information), reach (how widely the message is delivered) and price (the expense in time and dollars to deliver the message).

**Media coverage**, also called publicity, can consist of both traditional media (print, TV and radio), as well as digital media (internet). Media is a powerful promotional tool as it provides ample time to explain the product, wide reach and it delivers a message that is generally trusted by the consumer. Although some control is given up, the return can be significant. Pricing for publicity is variable. Most PR firms bill hourly whether or not publicity is obtained, making the expense a

risky endeavor. Media Relations Agency's Pay-Per-Interview Publicity® pricing model takes the gamble out of obtaining publicity.

**Websites** give you complete control of the message and ample bandwidth needed to tell your product's story. Of course, other promotions are needed to drive people to your website or even the best-produced website is ineffective. Consumer trust in websites is generally favorable, but can be enhanced by items such as media stories and customer endorsements.

**Social Media** is a good way to reach customers on a conversational level. Popular content can be passed along almost endlessly. However, posts of that caliber can be difficult to achieve.

**Advertising** has been around a long time and appears in many forms. Think of advertising as a parasite that attaches to a host. Ads attach themselves to magazine articles, newspaper stories, popular TV and radio programs, social media streams, websites, and even roadways in the form of billboards. Because ads are generally looked upon unfavorably by the public, people have conditioned themselves to skip over them.

This is commonly referred to as ad blindness. Today, because of the internet, ads can be both inexpensive and highly targeted.

**Personal selling** is an effective and often expensive way to deliver a promotional message. Although the message is under your control, believability is dependent on your salesperson: Is he/she seen as too slick or as a trusted professional? Because of the low reach and high expense, this method is best suited for big-ticket items where the market feels they need to speak with someone before they purchase.

Pros and cons of each of the channels:

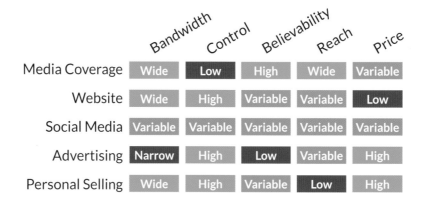

| | Bandwidth | Control | Believability | Reach | Price |
|---|---|---|---|---|---|
| Media Coverage | Wide | Low | High | Wide | Variable |
| Website | Wide | High | Variable | Variable | Low |
| Social Media | Variable | Variable | Variable | Variable | Variable |
| Advertising | Narrow | High | Low | Variable | High |
| Personal Selling | Wide | High | Variable | Low | High |

*A brand is the definition consumers hold in their minds of a company and its products. A brand is built in two ways: by what the customer is told, and by what the customer experiences.*

Think of a brand as a collection of senses and emotions in a consumer's mind that forms a concept associated with a product or organization. For example, a consumer may associate an upscale restaurant with delicious ingredients, a relaxing atmosphere, flattering service and expensive prices. The consumer has assembled these perceptions both by what he was told through marketing promotions and by dining at the restaurant. The integration of messages and experiences forms a concept in the consumer's mind.

The consumer may have a collection of images, smells, tastes and feelings in his mind when he thinks about the restaurant. It may take a few moments for him to explain his perception in words. If asked to define the restaurant, he may just say, "It's a nice restaurant" or "It's more upscale." But his collection of memories and associations, such as crisp salad, fragrant candles, smiling waiter and hefty bill, all help form in his mind as a concept. This concept is a brand.

In contrast to our definition, traditional definitions of the term "brand" are often more descriptive of a name or logo. Those definitions are lacking because they imply that people's perceptions come from a name or logo. However, names and logos do not create brands themselves. A logo is simply a visual cue to the puzzle pieces that create a brand in a consumer's mind: puzzle pieces such as the delectable taste of a restaurant's food, a co-worker's heartfelt recommendation of the pastry, or the classy background music in the dining area. Once a concept of an organization and its offerings has been formed in the consumer's mind, the brand exists as the definition of the organization's name and logo.

*The second step in the SAM 6 process is developing Code Sheets. Code Sheets are a means of gathering and documenting important information about your company and the products it promotes. Code Sheets can also be made for specific offers.*

*Code Sheets help direct and control your creative staff.*

Code Sheets document:

> The offering
> The company vision
> The company mission
> The market
> Key messages
> Positioning
> Brand statement

Code Sheets are based on the communication process: A sender encodes a message that is decoded by the receiver. Note that in the communication process, code is established prior to creating the message.

The code is like a framework around which all of your promotional messages are built. Each Code Sheet is a document created by management that gives clear direction to the creative team. Code Sheets help ensure that your messages are consistently focused for the best possible response.

One Code Sheet should be created for the company. In addition, one Code Sheet will be created for each product, and if the product has submarkets, one will be made for each submarket as well. Code Sheets can also be created for specific offers. For instance, if a special report is being offered or an event is being promoted.

Generally, Code Sheets should be shared with your creative team and are considered confidential. Like the Control Template in Step 5 of the SAM 6 process, Code Sheets are used both before a promotion is created and for evaluation before the promotion goes out.

Code Sheets take thought and time to develop, but this effort is worthwhile. They should be referred to regularly by your marketing team.

Sender → Encode → Message → Decode → Receiver

*In the Communication Process, a sender wants to communicate a message to a receiver. The sender encodes the message. Then the message is decoded by the receiver.*

Promotional communication can take many different forms; for example, it could be a package label, brochure, ad, blog post, tweet or jingle. Whichever form it takes, each element of the Communication Process can have a significant effect on your marketing strategy's success.

**Sender:** Consider who will deliver your message. For instance, will you use a key opinion leader, an anonymous writer or the CEO of your company?

**Code:** The code consists of the key messages you want to convey and how your offering differs from the competitors.

**Message:** Messages can be short like ads or long like media stories. So, sometimes your code will be stated briefly, maybe even in the form of bullet points. Other times, where you have more space, the code will be described in long winding stories.

**Decode:** No matter who your messenger is or the length of the message, the challenge is always to have the message decoded correctly. In other words, you want the receiver to make a meaningful connection to the main points you are trying to get across. The public may decode your marketing message differently than you planned. For example, marketers for a clothing store may run an ad that offers 30% off on select merchandise. "Discounted merchandise" could be interpreted in different ways by different people. College students may think discounted clothing means "inexpensive" or "affordable", while wealthy executives may consider discounted clothing "out of style" or "flimsy". This confusion could lead to unhappy customers or missed sales opportunities.

**Receiver:** The receivers—the people who receive your message—are often being distracted while your message is being conveyed. In addition, as the receiver takes in your message, the receiver's own beliefs and expectations can affect his or her understanding. The evidence of how the receiver decoded your message will show up in the resulting action they take.

*When marketers use promotions to support a company in general, it is commonly referred to as Institutional Advertising.*

Institutional Advertising is used to define the company in its entirety. When a company creates Institutional Advertising, the promotional message is directed at the entire market. When marketers create promotions, they need to consider whether they are trying to promote the company in general, or if they are trying to support a specific product or service.

When planning Institutional Advertising, marketers should take care to keep the message in sync with the company's vision and mission because when marketers promote the company in general, it has a "halo effect" on its individual products. For example, you wouldn't want a beverage company that produces healthy drinks to sponsor a hotdog eating contest. How the company portrays itself through Institutional Advertising will affect how customers perceive the company's products when they see it on the shelf.

*A company's vision defines how a company will look and what it will be in the future. It's what it one day intends to become. By definition, a company does not currently match its vision. Companies draft vision statements as a basis for aligning activities.*

For the purpose of marketing, Vision Statements should be kept short. Ideally, it will be no more than a concise phrase that people can easily understand, adopt and recall. The simpler the vision statement, the more likely it will be to stay on point and be achievable.

If a vision statement is too long, it is essentially worthless. You and the rest of your organization won't be able to remember it or keep it in mind as you move through the details of day-to-day life. Rather than serving as a quick and easy mental guidepost on which to base decisions, it will probably reside buried in a computer or gathering dust on a shelf.

Like a beacon on the hill, a company Vision is a landmark on the horizon for everyone to aim toward. Its purpose is to guide and inspire everyone's actions, big and small. Actions that will collectively take you to the place you would like the company to be.

*A company's mission is a statement that encapsulates HOW a company intends to achieve its vision.*

> **Vision Statement:** *This is what we are going to become.*

> **Mission Statement:** *This is how we are going to do it.*

There is interplay between the concepts of Company Mission and Company Vision.

A vision is a statement or description of what a company wants to become. A mission is the action that leads to the vision coming true.

When comparing vision, mission and daily activities, vision ranks at the top of the hierarchy. Then comes mission; the mission has to fit the vision. Then the company's daily activities need to pertain to the mission.

The company's daily activities cannot be just a random group of pursuits, running every which way. People within the company need to know the Company Mission, and be able to tell what fits with the mission and what does not. The mission should be one of the guideposts and measures for evaluating the activities pursued by the company.

A company may decide to have different versions of the same mission statement, using the same ideas but writing them out in longer or shorter lengths for different purposes. That's an option, but the company should still have a short version of the mission statement so that the people in the company can remember and therefore use it.

A concise, usable mission statement contributes to morale. Having a mission can confer a sense of meaning and direction. Employees benefit from feeling like they're a part of a mission and understanding how they fit into that mission. The more thoughtfully you choose and adhere to your mission statement, the better your organization will run.

*The third step in the SAM 6 process is selecting the appropriate Promotional Mix channels. The Promotional Mix channels you choose to employ depend on many variables including your message, the market and your resources.*

There are five channels in the Promotional Mix:

Publicity
Website
Social media
Advertising
Personal selling

The channels you choose to use depend on variables such as your message (which channels provide the bandwidth, believability and necessary control needed to share your message), the market (how engaged is your audience with the channel) and your resources (advertising, especially traditional ads, can be very expensive).

Selecting the right Promotional Mix will help you deliver your message effectively and efficiently, and will increase the likelihood of the receiver taking action.

Sometimes people jump to this third step without identifying the code, step two. This is a mistake. Knowing where your target market is most likely to engage favorably with your message will help you determine the appropriate channels to use. Think of the Promotional Mix as a variety of vehicles that will carry your message. While anything with wheels can get you from point A to point B, not all of them are right for your message. A sports car isn't going to transport a family of six to soccer practice nor is a used minivan the right car for a young professional looking to impress. And neither of these is the right vehicle for a farmhand hauling hay.

Take time to consider all aspects of the Promotional Mix channels as they relate to the many unique variables you are faced with.

*The Consumer Buying Process describes the steps that consumers go through as they decide whether to purchase and keep a product. This process follows a predictable pattern. Smart marketing will address the different steps in the Consumer Buying Process.*

Your organization needs to be aware of this process so you can apply marketing tactics to address consumers' mindsets at each stage, and help convince them to buy and keep your product.

There are five main steps in the Consumer Buying Process:

Needs Recognition

↓

Information Search

↓

Evaluation of Alternatives

↓

Purchase Decision

↓

Post-Purchase Behavior

Here's how each step is explained:

**Needs Recognition:** First, the consumer realizes that he has a need. Maybe his stomach is growling, and he realizes he needs lunch. Maybe his washing machine is leaking water all over the floor, and he needs to get it repaired. Or perhaps the relatives are visiting on Saturday, and he realizes that he will need to find an activity that they can all enjoy together.

**Information Search:** Almost immediately after the consumer realizes he has a need, his focus will switch to trying to find a solution. What can he do to address that need? For example, if he is hungry, what restaurants are nearby where he could buy lunch? If he needs an appliance repair company, what search terms can he use to find local repair companies online? If he needs to plan a family outing, what destinations are nearby?

**Evaluation of Alternatives:** Next, the consumer will narrow down his options to a few choices. For example, if the consumer needs to plan a family outing, he may consider such options as going to a movie, the zoo or an amusement park.

The consumer will weigh the pros and cons behind each option. He may really want to see a new adventure movie, but the weather could be beautiful that day and it would be shame to spend the pleasant afternoon inside of a darkened theater.

**Purchase Decision:** Then the consumer will make a choice. For example, he may decide to take his family to the zoo when they visit because the children will burn off lots of energy running between exhibits.

**Post-Purchase Behavior:** The purchase decision may be followed by buyer's remorse, also called cognitive dissonance. If the consumer decides to take his family to the zoo, he may feel a tinge of regret because he really wants to see the new adventure movie and doesn't know when he'll have time to see it otherwise.

Generally, the bigger the purchase, the stronger the buyer's remorse can be. If a consumer buys a candy bar from a vending machine and wonders if a Twix bar might have been better than the Snickers, the buyer's remorse will not be that significant. However, if a consumer buys a luxury car and then starts to wonder if the monthly payments are really affordable, the buyer's remorse will be stronger.

**Uses for Knowledge of the Consumer Buying Process:** When you know that people follow a predictable pattern in their buying process, you can address these stages. Let's take the example of a salesperson at a car dealer. Imagine that a consumer initially seems very determined to buy a new convertible. The consumer gives the salesperson her phone number and asks him to call when the new model arrives. When the salesperson first calls to tell her that the new model has arrived in the store, the consumer seems very excited. But then when the salesperson checks back with her a week later, she doesn't pick up the phone or return his voicemail. Being aware of the Consumer Buying Process, the salesperson will know it's possible that she is looking into other options (including convertibles at other dealerships).

You can use knowledge of the Consumer Buying Process to anticipate your competition. For example, if the salesperson suspects the consumer is in step 3. Evaluating Alternatives, the salesperson can bring up the likely competition and review the competitive differences. By calling attention to the alternatives before the consumer ever leaves the car dealership, the salesperson may prevent her from visiting the other dealers because she feels fully informed.

Remember that smart marketing will speak to all the steps of the consumer buying process. For example, to deal with step 5. Post-Purchase Behavior, businesses can prevent customers from returning a product by following up with letters or phone calls reassuring customers that they have made a smart purchase, reminding them of warranties that protect them, and demonstrating that the business has a history of standing behind their product.

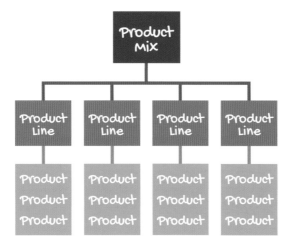

*The Product Mix is a table that categorizes a company's products into "product lines". Large companies with many products may have groups of lines called silos or platforms.*

Companies often have many products. The collection of products a company offers is called their Product Mix. The Product Mix can be organized as a table which categorizes similar products into "product lines". Large companies with many products may have groups of lines called silos or platforms.

If a company doesn't categorize its products and consider its Product Mix, confusion can result. Mentally keeping track of all of the company's products can be very challenging. Having a methodical system of organizing products is just much more efficient and easier to work with. In addition, once a company has organized its Product Mix and come up with a written system of categorization for its products, this categorization can be used across the company. Having these clear categories can speed internal communications.

For example, a chain of trendy women's clothing stores may offer a huge variety of merchandise to its customers. The people who manage the chain's new offerings need to keep track of all the merchandise by category, to make sure that each season they offer casual clothing, professional clothing, activewear and accessories. If management assembles a Product Mix table for the new season and notices that there are no new activewear styles, they can put more effort into that area.

Organizing your product mix in an understandable manner is very useful. A Product Mix table provides a nice an overview that will help point out opportunities as wells problems.

Something else the Product Mix might reveal is that some products or lines may not match the company's Vision or Mission. It's not unusual for companies to develop and entire division of products, only to sell it off when they realize the offerings are not in keeping with their core business.

Both large and small companies can benefit by thoughtfully organizing and evaluating their Product Mix.

# MARKETING SEGMENTATION STRATEGIES

*Markets can often be divided into segments of similar groups called submarkets. But how many submarkets should a market be divided into? Three? Eight? Fifty? None at all?*

*Consider these four strategies:*

**Undifferentiated targeting strategy:**
Using one promotional strategy for all marketing segments

**Concentrated targeting strategy:**
Tailoring promotions only to the most lucrative marketing segments

**Multi-segmented targeting strategy:**
Creating unique promotions to multiple market segments

**Micro-segmented targeting strategy:**
Marketing to each specific individual

## Undifferentiated

The undifferentiated strategy means that there is no market segmentation. The entire market is treated as one group. An undifferentiated strategy means everyone in your market gets the same message. Often times companies will use an undifferentiated strategy when creating messages that promote the whole company and use it in conjunction with another segmentation strategy when promoting specific products.

## Concentrated

With a concentrated segmentation strategy, you focus your resources on promoting one, two or three primary market segments that have the most potential value. For example, if you are selling futons, you may decide that college students and young professionals are the most likely population segments to buy your product. With a concentrated segmentation strategy, you would devote your advertising resources to the interests of college students and young professionals, not to parents or retirees.

## Multi-segmented

A multi-segmented strategy creates separate marketing messages for four or more different market segments. Because this strategy requires significant resources, it is often used by large companies who want to dominate a particular product category.

## Micro-segmented

A micro-segmented strategy targets marketing to a very small group of people, perhaps even all the way down to the individual level. For instance, online retailers may keep track of enough information about individual shoppers that they can promote products tailored to one shopper's personal tastes and habits.

Sometimes the idea of creating messages for different segments seems so attractive to marketers that it is easy to forget that additional segmentation consumes more resources. It is costly in money, time and labor to market separately to different segments. Before you get swept up in the idea of creating separate messages for different market segments, remember that it is only necessary to do so if a message that resonates with one part of your market doesn't resonate with another. As you identify different segments, make sure that you actually need to say something different to each segment. Otherwise, there's no reason to segment.

A possible starting strategy is to conserve resources by initially trying *not* to segment your market. Then if it becomes necessary, you can branch out into creating separate marketing strategies for different segments. If you decide that you need to segment your market, it will take discipline to carry out your plan. For example, if you sell fine handmade suits and decide that your advertising budget is best spent on a concentrated strategy playing to wealthy executives, you may have to exercise discipline to stick to your plan and not spend money on ads geared to entry-level professionals.

Choosing a Segmentation Strategy will help commit your resources to the market segments you have identified as the most valuable.

*Market Segmentation Variables are characteristics and elements used to build a profile or persona of a market. Here are some main categories:*

**Demographic:** *age, gender, income, ethnicity, family lifecycle.*

**Geographic:** *geographic location such as city, state, region, etc.*

**Psychographic:** *a mindset such as surfers, health conscious, political orientation, etc.*

**Geodemographic:** *combines psychographic and geographic, for example, New York business people think differently than Montana ranchers.*

**Benefit sought:** *low price, high quality, quick delivery, best color, etc.*

**Usage rate:** *frequent buyer, one-time buyer, sporadic buyer, moderate buyer, etc.*

Conceptualizing and building a profile of a target customer (to more effectively market to them), can be thought of as beginning with a stick person and adding characteristics from the Market Segmentation Variables until you form a comprehensive individual.

Understanding who a market is: how they think, where they live, what they value, etc. can help you create compelling examples in your marketing.

Once you have built a profile of your market using Segmentation Variables, you may want to give your market a name. If you determine the average age of your typical customer and know whether your product appeals more to a male or female, you can research common names for people of that age and gender. Using those names will help you build believable characters with whom your customers in that market segment can more easily identify. Moms who were born in the late 1970s may identify with other women named Amy or Jennifer, whereas their grandmothers may relate to women named Estelle or Dorothy.

**Seniors:** *Prior to 1945*

**Baby Boomers:** *1946 – 1964*

**Gen X:** *1965 – 1979*

**Millennials:** *1980 – 1994*

**Post Millennials or Gen Z:** *1995 – early 2000s*

Our brains become hardwired by the events that shape us. Often we develop mindsets that never really go away. Major external events can shape the personality traits of a generation, and these traits become deeply rooted.

As a marketer, you want to consider the traits of the generations to whom you are speaking. Rather than fighting against a generation's tendencies, address the generation's values and use terms they understand. For example, if you are trying to market your bank to teenagers, you will want to use social media ads to promote banking features that work well on smartphones.

Consider the reasons why certain generations have specific viewpoints. For example, if your travel agency is promoting tours to Vietnam, you will need to be sensitive to experiences that people from the baby boomer generation may have had during the Vietnam conflict. You would speak to baby boomers about touring Vietnam much differently than you would speak to recent college graduates.

When designing a promotional strategy, it is easy for marketers to make the mistake of thinking that everyone will think the way they do. It may be tempting to assume that everyone has the same impression of world events, jokes, technology or family roles. Remember that different generations have experienced certain events that have shaped their perceptions. Speak to them on their terms.

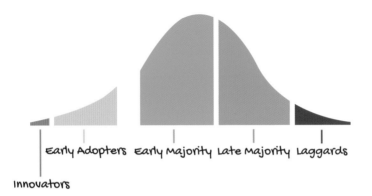

**Innovators:** *Immediately adopt and even think up new products and trends.*

**Early Adopters:** *Quick to adopt the products and trends. Little loyalty because their nature is to move on to new products and trends.*

**Early Majority:** *Open to trying some new products and trends but watch which way the wind blows before they decide. Not everything the early adopters do catches on with this group. They are loyal but open to change.*

**Late Majority:** *Skeptical. Will use products and trends only after they appear to be accepted by the mainstream. Loyal and slow to change.*

**Laggards:** *Hold on to the old and resist the new. Valued customers when a product is in the decline stage of the product lifecycle.*

Individual consumers adopt new products at different rates. In general, people think differently in terms of how quickly they will accept change. Consumers can be divided into five groups regarding how quickly they adopt new products. Those groups can be spread along a bell curve called the Innovation Adopter Curve.

It's important to understand the mindsets of each group along the Innovation Adopter Curve as you approach them to promote your product, service or offering. The same promotional messages will not appeal to each one so you need to adapt your message and use different marketing tactics that complement each group's willingness to adopt new products.

Except for Innovators, each group follows the lead of the group in front of it. Marketers should always be mindful of the next step in the Innovation Adopter Curve and consider how to help a product make the transition from one consumer group to the next.

People such as Innovators who are at the beginning of the curve tend to be wealthier and more highly educated. As the curve progresses, the people become less educated and have less disposable income. Early Adopters often purchase expensive new products even though they know they will be able to buy the same product at a much lower price in the not-too-distant future.

The five categories are explained as follows:

### 1.  Innovators
People who start new trends or are the first to try new products are called the Innovators. Innovators march to the beat of their own drums. They are not happy unless they are thinking up something new. The Innovators are at the very beginning of the bell curve, and tend to make up a very small percentage of the market.

### 2.  Early Adopters
Early Adopters watch what the Innovators are doing and pick up new trends quickly. Early Adopters love new products and share the Innovators' insatiable appetite for them.

As with the Innovators, Early Adopters display little loyalty to products because it is in their nature to move on to new offerings.

### 3.  Early Majority
Just as the Early Adopters watch the Innovators, people in the Early Majority watch the Early Adopters. Each group watches the group in front of them to see what they are doing before they adopt a product or trend. People in the Early Majority are more tentative about change. They think, "I see a lot of people doing this, so I'm going to do this, too."

People in the Early Majority are loyal to products in a way Innovators and Early Adopters are not.

### 4.  Late Majority
Consumers in the Late Majority tend to be harder to convince. They will use products and trends only after they appear to be accepted by the mainstream. Those in the Late Majority tend to be very loyal to products they have adopted and slow to change.

People in the Late Majority may finally think, "Okay, everybody's doing this, so I guess I should be too."

## 5.  Laggards

Laggards hold on to the old and resist the new. Laggards are a small group at the end of the bell curve. In a way, they are similar to the Innovators because they are outside of the mainstream, marching to the beat of their own drums.

## Inverse Relationship Between Innovation Adoption & Loyalty

There is an inverse relationship between a customer's speed in adopting new products and the amount of his or her loyalty.

For example, Innovators and Early Adopters have very little loyalty to a product. Although they are quick to try new products and will help bring a product to the market, they won't be loyal to a particular product. On the other hand, the Late Majority and Laggards may be very slow to start buying a new product, but once they adopt a product and are "hooked," they tend to be very loyal and will keep buying that product until they have a very good reason not to.

## A Marketer's Challenge

The challenge from a marketing perspective is to convince the Early Majority and Late Majority to adopt your product, service or offering. The Early Majority and Late Majority contain the largest numbers of consumers. And, the Early Majority and Late Majority tend to be more loyal to products than the Innovators and Early Adopters.

But, products will not necessarily be adopted throughout the Innovation Adopter Curve. As products move through the groups, there is a winnowing-out or culling process. With each successive group in the Innovation Adopter Curve, the fewer the number of products that get adopted. Only a few products will actually be accepted by the next group in the continuum. For example, Innovators may try 100 products, then Early Adopters may pick up 10 of them, and then the Early Majority may only adopt 3.

Marketers may be able to tempt Innovators and Early Adopters to try a new product, but getting the next stage, the Early Majority, to adopt the product is a different story. There is a jump that has to be made to get a product from the Innovators/Early Adopters to the Early Majority. Not all products can make this jump. Timing is also an issue; once the Early Adopters have stopped treating a product as new and exciting, the Early Majority will likely see this. The challenge becomes, how to bridge the gap between the Innovators/Early Adopters and the Early Majority.

A marketer needs to understand how the categories in the Innovation Adopter Curve think and behave.

Marketers should finesse their strategies as they try to move their product into the next category. Moving a product into the next category could require a change of key messages and/or a change in spokespeople. Language that appeals to the Innovators, such as "brand new" and "just released", might actually scare off the Late Majority. The Late Majority could be more attracted by the phrases "time-tested," "proven," "generally accepted," or "trusted." Likewise, a spokesperson who the Innovators know and like may not even be recognized by the Late Majority. To help their product be adopted by later stages of consumers, marketers will need to find spokespeople who are more relevant to the Late Majority.

## Summary

Leveraging the Innovation Adopter Curve boils down to three steps: Know that consumers adopt new products at different rates. Know that consumers can be categorized into groups related to how quickly they adopt new products. And know that promotional messages that are intriguing to one group may act as a warning flag to another.

*Primary Value Points are the top one, two or three (maybe as many as 5) reasons why consumers purchase a product. These should be prioritized in order of significance.*

*Secondary Value Points are all of the less common reasons people purchase a product.*

There are many different reasons customers buy a product. Once you create a complete list of those reasons they can be broken down into Primary and Secondary Value Points.

Primary Value Points are the main reasons why a consumer would purchase a product. These should be prioritized to ensure that the most significant points receive the most attention when creating promotional messages for a product.

Primary Value Points should be an integral part of all product promotions.

Secondary Value Points are less important, less common reasons people buy. Secondary Value Points are useful for augmenting a promotion. Sometimes they can be used as a novel introduction to the product. A consumer may purchase a new car primarily because it is safe, fuel-efficient and affordable. But they also like the color, the feel of the steering wheel, and the sound of the horn. Each of these reasons are worth mentioning but a marketer needs to make sure they give the most attention to the primary reasons their market considers when purchasing.

*The Unique Selling Proposition is a claim your product can make that none of your competitors can.*

The Unique Selling Proposition (USP) is the unique reason why your product is different and better than any others. Some USPs are very important to customers and some are less important. Consequently, some USPs will be Primary Value Points and some will be Secondary Value Points. Not every product will have a strong Unique Selling Proposition, but having one will help differentiate your product from the competition.

A Unique Selling Proposition (USP) could be related to a product's qualities, its price or even its location. For example, if you are selling a face cream and your product is the first in the marketplace to contain organic grapefruit oil, the unique ingredient and its benefits would be your USP. If you are a neighborhood ice cream shop, you may serve the same ice cream as other shops in town, but your USP may be that you are the only shop located in particular neighborhood, adjacent to a city park. These benefits are unique and differentiate your product from others in the marketplace.

Your USP is important because it provides you with leverage in the marketplace. One advantage when selling in a market where there are similar products — there are very few completely unique products — is the ability to identify and capitalize on your USP. Successful marketing using your USP will make your product stand out from the competition.

It is important to note that your USP isn't necessarily an indication of the best quality. Having the lowest price or being available at the closest location are advantageous USPs but say nothing about the quality of the product itself.

***The fourth step in the SAM 6 process is scheduling your promotions on a calendar.***

There are many variables to consider when filling in your calendar. Begin by determining which products will get the most attention and how often the organization in general will be promoted. You will also need to consider separate promotion for submarkets. Then determine how often you will cycle through your Primary Message Themes and Positioning as well as which Primary Message Themes will get the most attention. In addition, determine which promotional channels work best for delivering your promotions, and if you need to make any seasonal adjustments. Keep in mind: you are not drafting the content. You are just documenting products, value points, markets, channels and frequency.

It takes time and thoughtful consideration to build out a calendar, but it is very worthwhile. You will be referring to it regularly. Depending on your circumstances, you may decide to create your calendar one month, one quarter, or one year at a time.

It is important to note that changes to calendars are inevitable and expected. Opportunities or challenges will arise which may require you to modify your calendar. Competent marketers also regularly analyze the effectiveness of promotions which should influence your calendar. Naturally, you will want to increase the use of the promotions which trigger the most conversions.

*Positioning is how your product is positioned in the mind of the consumer compared to the competition.*

Wouldn't it be nice if your product was the only one of its kind on the market? But it's probably not. Consumers almost always have the option of choosing between many competing products. Your product is Positioned in relationship to competitors' products. For example, when consumers consider purchasing new tires for their car, they may think, "Brand X is more expensive so it must be higher quality than brand Y." Positioning helps clarify your product's place in the market. Positioning also involves understanding the niche or void that your product fills.

Some factors that may be a part of your product's Positioning include:

Price
Quality
Speed of delivery
Convenience

Your product cannot be everything to everyone. For example, your product can't be an inexpensive yet high-end luxury home. Nor can it be a seven

passenger compact car. Positioning helps identify where your product fits into the array of the choices available.

Many times, consumers will be looking for a product with certain Positioning. For example, if a customer needs shoes to wear during a home renovation product, she may be specifically looking for footwear that is durable enough to protect her feet from debris but also cheap enough to discard if they get covered with paint. The customer may just want a generic, affordable pair of shoes that have utility value. They do not need to be on-trend. If a shoe manufacturer wants to position itself in this practical-thinking portion of the market, the manufacturer will want to keep down costs and not spend extra money adapting to short-lived trends.

*A Brand Statement is a short paragraph written in the words a customer would use if you overheard them describing your product to another person, and they got it exactly right.*

When formulating your Brand Statement, it may be helpful to consider what it would sound like if you overheard one coffee shop patron talking to another about your product, and they accurately explained your product in their own words. That is your Brand Statement.

The building blocks of your Brand Statement are found on your Code Sheets and they are the Primary Value Points and Positioning.

For example, if the product is dog food, the Primary Value Points might be that it smells appealing to dogs, is easily digested, and comes packaged in individual serving packets. Its positioning could be that it is formulated and named after leftovers such as leftover turkey dinner or leftover chicken salad.

In that case, the Brand Statement might be written like this: *I bought this new dog food and my dog just loves it. He was always a picky eater but not anymore. He goes nuts as soon as he gets a whiff of this stuff. And, you know how dogs love table scraps? Well, XYZ company came up with flavors based on the popular meals people eat – like Leftover Turkey Dinner and Day Old Lasagna. And this may sound silly but I think my dog now has more regular bowel movements. Another thing I like about it is the food comes packaged in individual serving sizes based on the dog's weight. You should try it for your dog.*

*A - Attention*
*I - Interest*
*D - Desire*
*A - Action*

*The acronym AIDA is a classic, time-honored format that can be followed to create an effective promotional message. AIDA is a helpful tool for producing promotional communications that will be compelling to consumers.*

Here is an explanation of the AIDA steps:

### Attention

The first AIDA step is to capture the audience's attention. How you attract the audience's attention does not necessarily have to do with the message you will be subsequently trying to convey. For example, a professor who wishes to gain her students' attention may begin class by dropping a heavy textbook on the classroom floor, making a loud thud. The students will probably be surprised and alert to whatever the teacher says next. Dropping a textbook on the floor may not have anything to do with the message trying to be conveyed in the lecture, but it has definitely has gotten the students' attention.

### Interest

The next AIDA step is to build interest. The point is to keep the audience engaged. Building interest is part of the process of winning over the audience.

### Desire

Desire is the most difficult step in AIDA. As a marketer, you need to convince consumers to desire what you're offering more than whatever they must give up to get it. If you are creating promotions for the purpose of gathering leads and contact information, the customer normally has to give you some of their time and energy, so the bar is set fairly low. If on the other hand your promotion is trying to make a sale, the bar is set much higher. People have a very strong desire to keep their money. Getting them to desire your product more than their money is a difficult challenge.

### Action

Your final goal is for consumers to take action. The action may be to buy your product, call a representative, or navigate to your website. There are tactics that encourage consumers to take action. One technique is to carefully spell out and encourage exactly what you want them to do.

For example; *Give us a call. You will never have to wait on hold because we have people standing by to answer your call. You can ask them any question you like and they will never pressure you to purchase. On average we have found that calls are completed in 4 minutes. Should you purchase our product, our shipping department is set up to get all orders processed and shipped within 24 hours. We use two-day shipping, so you can expect your product will arrive within three days. Should you be unhappy with the product we include a post paid return envelope, even though our return rate is less .001 percent.*

By the time you get to the Action point of your promotion, the consumer is at a tipping point of completing a purchase. Consequently the nudge could be quite small. Coupons can be one such tactic. If a grocery store hangs a coupon for even a small discount next to the item on a shelf, this could be enough justification to convince a consumer to buy that product instead of another.

*Feature: a distinctive attribute or aspect*

*Benefit: an advantage gained from something*

*Desire: a strong feeling of wanting something or wishing for something to happen*

Features, Benefits and Desires are an important combination in marketing. A Feature is a part or aspect of a product, such as an auto-programming Feature on a coffee maker.

The Benefit is what that Feature can do for you. For example, the Benefit of the coffee maker's auto-programming Feature is that it can have your coffee ready for you when you wake up in the morning.

Desire is longing to have that Feature and Benefit. For example, you may Desire smelling hot coffee when you awaken, and you may Desire being able to drink the coffee right away without waiting for it.

Marketers use the combination of Feature, Benefit and Desire to sell a product. Consider the example of a sweater in a clothing store during winter. A Feature of the sweater is that it is thickly woven with soft yarn. A Benefit of the sweater is that it helps keep you warm in the cold wind. A Desire that a shopper may have is to wear the sweater because it feels cozy and would look stylish.

Marketers may design advertisements that show a model wearing the sweater while happily drinking cider around a campfire with good-looking companions. The advertisements play to a shopper's Desire to look good while staying warm.

A common sales model is to state a Feature and then explain how the Feature will Benefit the customer. That can be helpful, but also consider that sometimes a customer may have a Desire to buy a product and use the Features to justify that Desire. For example, a customer may Desire to buy a certain recreational boat. The customer may dream of floating on a luxurious boat on a beautiful summer afternoon, enjoying the sunshine and sipping a cold drink with friends. In his heart of hearts, the customer realizes that the boat is very expensive. But the brochure may point out that the boat utilizes new environmentally friendly technology and that its engine is extremely fuel efficient. The the customer may use the environmentally friendly technology and fuel efficiency as a way to rationalize buying the boat. He may tell himself that he is encouraging the development of "green" technology and saving the environment by buying the boat. In this case, the customer is using a Feature to justify his Desire.

Marketers should be aware of just how important a customer's Desire can be. Marketers should make sure that their promotions play to customers' Desires.

The Feature/Benefit/Desire concept is related to the AIDA (Attention, Interest, Desire, Action) concept in that both show the importance of creating Desire in a customer.

*The fifth step in the SAM 6 process is developing a control template for your creative team. Your control template provides the guidelines for your writers, designers and other creative staff to follow. The control template allows these imaginative professionals to create attention-getting content without losing site of the marketing necessities.*

A control template can be modified to meet your needs, but these are some key elements:

Mission and Vision
Product
Market
Primary Message Theme(s)
Sender
Channel

Seed Content
Keyword
Geography
Content Length
WIFM
AIDA

Much of the Control Template information is filled in from earlier steps, such as the product and primary message themes from your Code Sheets, or the channel from your calendar. Other components help your creative team produce the most effective content. For example, identifying the sender lets your creatives incorporate a unique voice or image. Including the keywords necessary for SEO or hashtags for social media help them create searchable content.

The content itself is written into the AIDA section of the Control Template. AIDA—Attention, Interest, Desire and Action—is a helpful tool for writing marketing prose.

Don't mistakenly think that this template will restrict creativity. It actually does the opposite. It eliminates uncertainty which causes tension and stress. It's hard to produce good creative work if you are guessing at what the other person wants.

*The Product Lifecycle is the period of time a product exists in the marketplace from its introduction to its discontinuation.*

*The Product Lifecycle consists of four stages:*

> *Introductory*
> *Growth*
> *Maturity*
> *Declining*

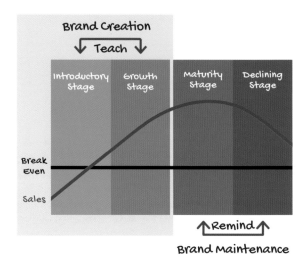

Although this is a general pattern, that does not mean that each and every product will move along this same lifecycle arc. The length of time that a product remains in each phase can differ greatly. For example, one product may take years to finally catch on, and just as it does, another product is introduced to the market that makes it obsolete within the next six months. Another product may catch on quickly and enjoy ten or twenty years of market dominance before it begins to decline.

The Product Lifecycle is important because how you market a product depends on where it is positioned in the Product Lifecycle.

## Introductory and Growth Phase Marketing

While a product is in the Introductory or Growth phase, Reach and Teach marketing tactics should be used. This focuses on creating the brand by educating consumers about the product: how it solves a frustration, what it can do and why it is needed. To be effective, techniques must both explain the product and encourage consumer listening. The product's story can be told via traditional media sources such as television, radio, magazines and newspapers and/or through digital tactics such as websites and social media. The key is to adequately explain the product and to present it in a format to which the consumer will be receptive. Media coverage is highly effective during these stages.

## Maturity and Declining Phase Marketing

Products in the Maturity or Declining phase of the Product Lifecycle should utilize Reach and Remind marketing tactics. Here the focus is on maintaining the brand by keeping the product top-of-mind for consumers. At this point, consumers are already aware of the product's benefits and a simple short reminder of the product is all that is needed to promote sales.

Advertising can be effective at this point. Any public relations tools used earlier must be modified to continue to engage the now-informed consumer.

A common mistake made by many businesses is to ignore the Product Lifecycle and promote a product using the same tools and tactics during all stages of the product lifecycle.

A word of caution: Since advertisements for popular products in the mature stage are ubiquitous, it is easy to be fooled into thinking that simply advertising a new product in the same way will encourage sales. Instead, the product can fail because consumers remain unaware of the benefits and/or solutions the product can offer. It's a mistake to use Reach and *Remind* tactics when Reach and *Teach* tactics should be used.

*Push strategy:* *Promotions within the distribution channel that cause consumers to be aware of the product. Example: a distributor offers retail stores a free boat they can use as a giveaway promotion if they buy a pallet of product and display it in the boat in their store.*

*Pull strategy:* *Promotions directed right to the consumer. This causes customers to go to the store and buy the product or ask the stores to stock it if they don't already. Consumer demand can cause a store to stock a product. This happened when we had an article run for Breathe Right Nasal Strips in an area where Target didn't stock them. Target was flooded with requests, so they began stocking the product.*

Push and Pull Marketing Strategies deal with whether a product is "pushed" to retailers and therefore to consumers, or whether promotions cause consumers to go to retailers and request a product, therefore "pulling" it into the market.

Push and Pull Marketing Strategies can be used simultaneously or individually.

*The Marketing Environment consists of factors that are beyond your company's control, such as the economy, the competition's technology level, major weather disturbances or world events. Marketers cannot control everything that happens in the outside world. Instead, they must understand how the external environment is changing and how that change will impact the market.*

As a business or other organization, you may feel driven to understand or predict all of the factors at play in your work. You can outline and plan many aspects of your organization, but no matter how much you try to keep your business under control, there will still be some variables that are simply out of your hands. You won't be able to prevent tropical storms from hitting the coastline, security threats from shutting down airports, or popular musical acts from setting new fashion trends.

When dealing with your marketing environment, remember two things:

**Don't bury your head in the sand.** Look around at new developments in the world, even if they seem unrelated to your product. Take a breather and observe which way the wind is blowing. Trends and world developments may affect your business more than you think.

**Recognize which factors in your marketing environment you can adapt to and which ones you can't.** For example, if you are producing a home improvement trade show and your food vendors' historically high prices are giving your event a bad reputation, maybe you can work with your vendors to change this. But if the stock market crashes and home values plummet, your home improvement trade show may not be of interest to consumers or exhibitors, and there is simply nothing you can do to change that.

One external element that you may not be able to control is the customer. Try as you might to influence the customer, if they don't want to buy cod liver oil, they won't buy cod liver oil. Whether the customer is right or wrong in their beliefs, continually hitting them with your promotions may not work. You need to understand your customer and be in touch with technological and cultural trends.

"Marketing environment" is a broad term that you may not utilize every day in your business, but is beneficial to consider from time to time. It's easy to be focused on day-to-day operations; remember to take some time to observe what is occurring in the world around you.

> **Reach:** *The size of the target audience exposed to a message.*
>
> **Frequency:** *Number of times the target audience is exposed to a message.*

When considering Reach and Frequency, marketers ask, how many people are we reaching and how many times do those people need exposure to that message?

Reach refers to the number of people who receive a message. For example, if you run an ad on a radio show with 500,000 listeners, the ad has a Reach of 500,000.

Different communication avenues can have huge differences in their Reach. For example, the Reach of a small-town newspaper, read by a limited number of local residents, is vastly different from the Reach of a national newspaper with potentially millions of readers.

Frequency refers to the amount of times people receive the message. If you run an ad 60 times on the radio, the ad has a Frequency of 60.

Frequency deals with the fact that just because you deliver your message to an audience once, that does not mean that they all saw it, or the ones who saw it remember it. You may have to repeat a promotional message many times before a substantial percentage of the audience retains it.

Consumers remember messages presented through some channels of the Promotional Mix better than they remember messages presented through others. For example, consumers may remember a product discussed on a television news program more than they remember information from an ad they flick past in their Facebook news feed.

In either case, it's highly unlikely that 100 percent of the audience will see your promotion. Not every person who subscribes to the magazine reads every article and not every person on Facebook notices every ad.

*The sixth step in Strategically Aimed Marketing involves your creative team. You need to assemble the right people for the job, and then let these creative souls work their magic within the parameters you set. The composition of your creative team will depend on your calendar.*

Some companies start with the creative process. But as you now understand, that's short-sighted. Regardless of the talent of your creative team, they will do a much better job if you first complete steps one through five.

Every company is going to require a different combination of creative talent at different times. It's not as easy as plugging in one full-time writer and one part-time designer or hiring a single Jack-of-all-trades.

Here are a few questions to get you thinking about creative talent:

**Q: Are you sharing your message through social media?**

A: You need a writer who excels at short, punchy content and a graphic designer who has an eye for the internet. You can't afford to be stale in that venue.

**Q: Marketing through emails?**

A: You'll need a persuasive writer and a marketing specialist.

**Q: Sharing white papers and factual content through your website?**

A: You'll need a creative team that specializes in this format and has technical skills such as search engine optimization.

**Q: Decide you need media coverage?**

A: You'll need a publicist with a long list of contacts.

When you add up your needs, you'll probably discover that it's fairly large and varied. Most companies find they don't have the ongoing need (or budget) to hire full-time internal staff with all of the creative skills required. That's why many companies decide to outsource some of their creative work to agencies, like ours.

*Sales Oriented: Aggressive selling like an MLM*

*Societal Oriented: Focus on doing good and giving back*

*Production oriented: Focus on efficiencies - leads to lower prices*

*Market Oriented: Focus on individual needs - leads to higher prices*

A company's marketing can have four orientations:

Sales
Societal
Production
Market

Consider ranking your orientation toward each of the four categories on a scale of one to ten. You will notice that, at least to some degree, you are oriented toward each one.

The orientations are explained as follows:

**Sales:** A company that is highly oriented toward Sales will be insistent and assertive with its selling tactics. For example, a company selling hand lotion through mall kiosks might instruct each salesperson to grab a passerby by the hand, apply a hand lotion sample and not let go of the person's hand until the sales pitch is over. A different company might find such a pushy sales tactic inappropriate for the brand it is trying to create. It may prefer to have its hand lotion sitting on a shelf in a popular, upscale salon where it is tactfully suggested by an accomplished stylist.

**Societal:** Companies with a high Societal orientation feel compelled to give back. They frequently support charities and non-profit organization with both money and labor. They are proud of their socially conscientious actions which are a natural part of the company's DNA.

Other companies may not do pro bono work, but rightly feel that providing quality products and creating jobs satisfies their Societal orientation.

By default, all companies and products are socially oriented to some degree because they all cater to a human need or want.

**Production:** A company that has a high Production orientation has the mindset of doing a few things well and beating its competition with low prices achieved through economy of scale. It gives little consideration to the whims and notions of individuals, preferring to create low-cost products that appeal to the masses. For example, if a Production-oriented company is selling children's art supplies, it is likely to provide a limited selection. Its tubes of glitter may consist of only gold and silver rather than an array of 28 different colors. The belief is that the market would prefer a limited selection at a lower price.

**Market:** A company with a high Market orientation values its customers' advice when deciding what products it should produce. It not only welcomes customer feedback, it seeks it out. For example, if a Market-oriented company is selling children's art supplies, it may conduct focus groups of parents and children. It may ask questions about how families choose their crayons, markers and glitter. It would then try to produce art supplies that fit the research data. Producing art supplies that match the nuanced needs of many customers can be costly. It's far less expensive to produce a plain blue crayon than a seabreeze-scented ocean-blue crayon with sparkles.

The "holy grail" in business is to provide each customer with exactly what he or she wants. However, customers may not necessarily be willing or able to pay the price for purchasing products tailored to their specific need.

## Tensions Between Marketing Orientations

Notice that while none of the categories are opposites of the others, there is tension between Sales and Societal as well as Production and Market. Companies that exhibit aggressive sales tactics tend to have a lesser Societal orientation, and companies that are highly Market-oriented will be less Production-oriented.

A common business mistake is trying to be a low price, Market-oriented company. It's nice to imagine that you can respond to a customer's every whim and still keep prices low, but the work this will require probably makes competing on price unrealistic.

That's not to say companies can't utilize a little of two competing orientations, such as being both a little Production-oriented and a little Market-oriented. A company could also be Market oriented with one product and Production oriented with another.

Marketing orientations can also change. During a recession, a company may adjust its focus to be more Sales-oriented and less Societal-oriented.

It is beneficial for a company to be aware of these orientations and know which point they occupy on the sliding scales. Understanding and embracing an orientation can help a company consciously develop its brand and marketing strategy.

# MARKETING TERMS

Find us at **www.publicity.com**

or give us a call at **952-697-5200**